SPIRIT BEACH

Sands of Serenity

Jay Morrow

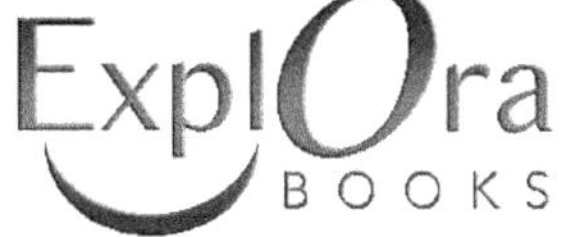

SPIRIT BEACH

"Sands of Serenity"

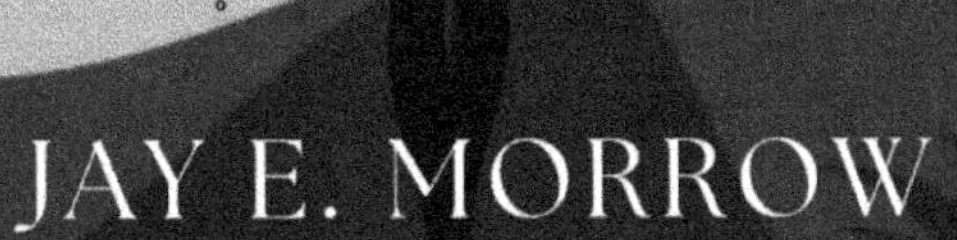

JAY E. MORROW

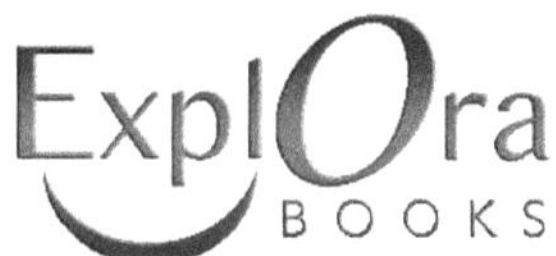

EXPLORA BOOKS
700 – 838 West Hastings St. Vancouver, BC V6C 0A6
www.explorabooks.com
Phone: (604) 330 6795

ISBN: 978-1-998394-11-1 (eBook)
ISBN: 978-1-998394-10-4 (Paperback)

Contents

The Professor

Professor Ray Durant sat in his borrowed chair, at his borrowed desk in his borrowed office and reflected upon his life. He looked down the length of both walls and saw a comforting sight, his beloved books. His steel grey eyes perused the shelves. As he stood up and examined some of the older books, which told of devilfish (Octopus) and sea wolves (Orca) he realized that during his lifetime how much had been learned about the coastal environments and its inhabitants.

He loved to bring examples of past thought into the classroom to let his students become aware that conventional wisdom was not always correct and to constantly challenge what was believed to be true until it was proved to be true. He even found his first dissertation on the interaction between predators and prey in beach environments. He grabbed the slim booklet and reclined in the artificial leather chair and put his feet up on the trash can. He laughed at how serious he had been back then and how young. His black hair had turned grey at the temples and he had grown intolerant of the politics of any large institution. But it also brought crashing back to him how he had been essentially cashiered by his school's administration. Although, at this point in his life, he had no need for the paycheck, the new Dean had been one of his students many years ago and his betrayal had hurt in many ways. The hue and cry on his termination for mere age had led the Dean to acquiesce to a series of lectures to be given once each year by Professor Durant on an emeritus position.

Just the thought of how he had been treated by the Dean of the school he loved, turned him another direction. He looked out the window overlooking Lake Union and just watched the numerous boats heading both directions, some to the Sound, some into the gentler limitations of Lake Washington. Lake Union was a natural link between the lake and its confines and the sea. He loved to watch the myriad of boats heading in and out of the locks and the lake. But finally, his thoughts turned to the Dean of the school and that deep inside how he was such a cold-hearted man.

The Dean was a short weasel-like sort of man, that the professor had tried in vain to introduce a passion for the material, but the

Dean just wanted to know what it would take to get an "A". In other words, the Dean, as a student was bright and industrious, but not driven by any special need to comprehend. His forte was politics and he had quickly risen to the heights of his station. In fact, many people had misinterpreted his appearance3 with a lack of social skills. They were very rudely surprised to find their careers shortened or terminated by the Dean's cunning use of politics and persuasion. His path to the top was strewn with the careers of many of the oceanologists that had not paid him what he considered to be the proper respect and deference. Now, as the head of the department, the Dean's idea of a successful staff, was not those which taught the best, but those who had published or brought in endowments for the school. Professor Durant had found himself at odds on many occasions, and was not surprised when the new rule concerning age had forced his retirement of his teaching position.

Although the Dean and his new administration at the University had made the decision to forcibly retire him several months ago, using a little-known requirement of publishing every five years or obtaining grants for research. Professor Durant had just lost his wife and was forced to concentrate most of his remaining energies on teaching and lecturing. Several of his peers learned of the Dean's plan and contacted the University hierarchy concerning other options. Originally, they were ignored; but they helped organize such a hue and cry from all his peers and his students. This included a series of protests and angry petitions from his students that had finally forced the Dean to suggest a compromise to his original position and bring him back as a Professor Emeritus for a series of lectures, each year. Although it had not affected his confidence in his own abilities, the effort of fighting the process had aged him and added some steel gray to his temples. The Dean had also demanded pre-approval of his subject matter. The professor hated that kind of censorship, and had ultimately refused. After several months of tense negotiations, the Dean had finally agreed to allow him carte blanche on his subject matter for a reduction in his honorarium.

Although his face was lined with the years of effort to transmit his knowledge to his students, he still maintained his clear steely blue and deep-set eyes, cleft chin and an aging athletic body. And it was not unusual for female students to become caught up in his charisma and try to "get to know him better". Something he always refused but was still flattered by their adulation, especially after his wife passed on. His predilection was for more experienced and mature partners. He had learned long ago that he was most attracted to those which loved the dance and byplay of romance versus a quick interchange of sex.

For years he had been known as one of the premier national experts on the interrelationships between marine animals and their habitat, and his classes had been one of those requirements for students who wished to be at the peak of understanding of marine biology or oceanography. But before he had always been reticent about talking about what drove him so hard in his chosen profession, because he was afraid of appearing crazy. But looking back at his relationship with his muse he decided to put all his fears aside. He began preparing for the most important series of lectures in his life. For the next two weeks, he would concentrate on putting into words the story of the most significant relationship in his life, how it had changed him, shamed him and led him into the decision to champion efforts to reduce the impact of humankind on the environment. remembered back to his first time on the Beach, when he was five. He took down a single sheet of paper and began to outline the story of his love for Sophia. He stared at the blank page for several minutes, until he said "What the Hell" and decided to tell what she told about herself when they first met, along with his favorite story that she had told him; concerning how she came to be the spirit and soul of the beach.

As he stared at his initial outline for his lectures, he finally decided to start with the spirit that had first moved him to dedicate his life to the study of the beach and its life. Once he decided to tell the full story, he knew he would have to discuss his "meme" and her story in more detail. He would have to describe what he knew of her origins and the story that she had told him over many years. He would introduce her in his lectures with how she began her life on the beach. Thus, we can now learn the story of "Sophia".

Sophia

Sophia had awakened after years of what had seemed like sleep. The feeling that the weight of thousands of pounds of glacial ice covering her was finally beginning to melt and retreat from the deep valleys it had cut, awakened her to the glories of her home. As the ice retreated and animals began to take possession of the beach, she grew stronger with each passing decade. She became the Spirit she was; full figured, womanly, and glowing with an internal fire. As life grew to inhabit the shore where the water remained in constant contact with the land, her powers grew. As the spirit of the Sound, she took up residence along a pristine shoreline on the Western shore.

Thus, for many years her strength and image matured. She was like but not like the first human inhabitants of the area. Her garments were originally made from the marine growths along the shore; clam shells, kelp, and seaweed soften her aspect and enhanced the loveliness of her curves and gave a hint of glories just barely hidden by the materials. She eventually designed a soft wrap made from materials which had washed up upon her domain, lost from some strange overseas environment.

Each year, the shoreline would increase the number and variety of organisms, and her strength grew proportionately. Clams, barnacles, crabs, sea-stars, snails, and fish made up the great preponderance of the growth, but even niche organisms added to her power as she blossomed into a beautiful and magnificent Spirit.

As she walked along her shores one day, she saw two eye stalks looking at her from the waves caressing the eel grass.

She looked directly at them and communed with Crab for the first time. "Hello" she said. "Come walk and talk with me".

At this invitation Crab walked out of the surf sideways, keeping an eye on her at all times. He said, "I see you here often as do some of my friends, who are you?"

"I am Sophia and what is your name?" He heard her voice in his head as if it were echoing in his small brain.

"Just call me Crab." was his response as his eyestalks rotated to keep watch behind him.

She had been watching him closely and was wondering what he was dragging behind him. Gradually it occurred to her that it was the rotting carcass of a flounder. Trying hard to hide her disgust she asked, "Who are your friend?

"Well, I have many among my own kind, but I talk and spend a lot of time with Octopus, Eagle and Raven" he responded quickly. "Eagle and Raven have been watching you for some time and say that you are a goddess, is that true?" Crab asked.

"I guess, whatever that means." was all she said.

He had noticed her staring at the flounder he was chewing on and so offered. "Well, let's do lunch sometime" which was Crabs favorite activity in all the world.

She hid her emotions and said "Yes, let's". But Sophia, who was totally unused to conversation at all, was a little taken aback. Before she could continue and ask when or where, crab disappeared under the waves. She could just barely see his eyestalks peering out of the eel grass watching her.

Sophia thought about this discussion for several weeks. She walked the same stretch of beach every day, but did not see the crab again. After living alone for eons, the ability to communicate with another sentient being was a complete shock, but one she enjoyed immensely. She desired desperately to do it again. One day, she looked over at a cedar tree which overhung the beach and saw a raven watching her. She remembered that crab had said the Eagle and Raven had been studying her for some time. So, she decided to try and get a response.

"Hello, why are you staring at me?" she inquired

"I have never seen a Spirit before and you are absolutely gorgeous to watch" he
replied. "Crab said you were easy to talk with too!"

"I only met Crab once, but I was intrigued by his offer to do lunch" she responded.

Raven chuckled, "Crab is a stomach on legs, so I'm not surprised. He is always dragging something to our meetings. Be careful and don't eat what he eats; he picks up all kinds of carcasses and just chomps away at them. He is not a proponent of the finer things in gastronomy."

"Thanks, for the warning! But when can I meet you and your friends? flounder I am lonely for a chance to talk about life and what I am doing here." she pleaded

"We are meeting tomorrow, at this very Cedar. Come at high tide, so Crab and Octopus don't have to walk far" he suggested and then flew off the limb and disappeared into the trees.

Sophia was at the appointed spot early. She saw octopus crawl out of the surf wearing her very best color, a soft purplish tone used to display openness and welcome. Octopus waved her front two tentacles in greeting.

Octopus began the conversation with "Hello, you must be Sophia".

Sophia responded with a welcome of her own and curtsied to the cephalopod.

Raven and Eagle arrived simultaneously from opposite directions. They were friends in this group, but not known to associate amicably at any other times. Even now, they landed on two different limbs of the cedar tree.

Last to arrive was crab; who of course was dragging a piece of barely recognized rockfish with him. As crab sat down, he chomped away at the piece of fish and offered Sophia a choice portion with a hearty "Wanth thum?"

After seeing the condition of the rock cod, Sophia politely declined his offer.

As they all sat down, Raven spoke as he usually did for the group. He was the most articulate, because Crab usually had some food hanging from its mouth which tended to garble his speech.

Raven started with "We have been guardians of this beach for many years, why should we allow you to take responsibility for any protections we currently offer?"

Just as Sophia started to answer, a low rumble was heard behind her. For the past ten days, rains had been saturating the lands away from the beach. As they all looked up

at the cliff, they saw the soil break away and a huge landslide slid remorsefully forward.

A quick decision had to be made, or they would all be buried under tons of soil. The animals froze in their locations, unsure of what to do and watched as Sophia turned towards the hillside. When the soil reached the large cedar, it shook and began to fall. Seeing that something had to be done, she gathered all her power; reached out and grabbed the trunk with both hands and held it as a bulwark against the onrushing soil. She struggled to hold the trunk as her feet slid over the beach rocks. Finally, her toes reached the hardened clay layer and dug into the immovable grey clay and she was able to stop the huge tree from toppling onto them. The cedar stopped at an angle, and its gigantic root-ball diverted the slide.

Octopus and Crab crawled back to the protective water while Eagle and Raven took flight and escaped. From this point on, Sophia could do no wrong in their eyes. And she could not go anywhere without one or all of these providing a watchful and protective eye for her safety. Although she felt safe under their protection, she also realized that after her display of strength, they no longer regarded themselves as her equals. They deferred to her in all decisions. She missed the give and take of having friends versus worshippers.

After centuries, the spirit that was Sophia and her friends began to notice a new entity enter the Sound, a new race called "human beings". Initially they were small band or families, but as they settled along the shorelines, they grew into large and sophisticated tribes. One day a canoe approached the beach; it was carrying a lone human being. He pulled the canoe up on the beach and began to build a fire and to chant in a low serious voice. He spoke of his tribe and their need for wisdom. nothing, and Sophia realized that he was on some sort of spirit quest.

The human ate She came to him at the end of day, and although his eyes widened at her beauty, he took her appearance in stride. They communed for hours about life and love and the meaning of it all. She showed him the bounty which was beneath her waters. The shaman's tribe had been living off the largesse of the salmon runs and ate a diet of vegetation, and dried, smoked or freshly cooked salmon. Sophia showed him where the clams were buried, how to catch crabs and the myriad of other fish which floated in her tide pools. The shaman took this learning and decided he needed to return to his tribe and show them the variety of marine life which was available to augment their diet.

One day as she came to his camp, his canoe was gone and the embers of his fire cold. She immediately felt the loneliness descend upon her again, as she missed their sharing of thoughts. He never returned and her loneliness and isolation deepened.

Now, it had been many years since the shaman of the Suquamish tribe had spent the week with her on a vision quest. A new race came to her shores. The coming of the white man brought a different kind of people and she perceived their greed for material things.

She saw that compared to the shaman the new arrivals did not believe in her as a Spirit. They understood only what could be grasped in their hands. She saw this as a double-edged sword. That although they had cut and removed trees, they also left many logs along her shores as new areas for life to grow and take root. For years, she sensed their greed about the life along her shores, but their take was minimal in comparison to the moon snails or starfish. Also, after the shaman no longer came along her shores, it had been too long with no one to talk with and share her own visions, she was looking for answers. The members of her bodyguard treated her not as an equal, but as the Spirit she was. The shaman had mentioned that he had also journeyed to the realm of the Mountains and had learned of a great king there.

Her First Tale

He had started out his lectures with his basic philosophy concerning the interrelationship of organisms in their environment. He had moved into a description of Sophia to give the audience a grasp on his motivation to learn about the beach environment in his youth that led to his many discoveries later in life. As the professor leaned back into the comfort of his writing chair, he decided that before he went any further, he needed to explain how he learned of conflict and the dangers associated with trying to control everything around you. She had taught him with a gentle story of how she grew to confront the other great spirit of the Northwest, the Mountain King. He was dangerous to all humans in the area, because he could actually destroy mountains and shake the earth. This is also his tale.

Tormented by her loneliness, Sophia decided to journey to the realm of the "Mountain King". He lived on the most beautiful of the seven pillars of fire which were near the Sound.

She asked Raven, Eagle, Octopus and Crab to accompany her as her personal bodyguard. Initially, they were resistant since Raven and eagle were not enamored of each other and crab and octopus actually preferred to eat each other. The Eagle and the Raven constantly argued with each other and crab and octopus kept a wary eye on where the other was, but their love for Sophia, overcame these obstacles and they agreed to accompany her on her quest.

As she flew with the Eagle and her bodyguards, they saw the magnificent edifice of the "Mountain King". It was almost translucent and shone in the early morning sunlight like an exquisite pearl. It was surrounded by forests and had a magnificent and unobstructed view of the surrounding area, including Sophia's beach.

She found the "Mountain King" resting in his splendid mountain ice palace. He had seen her from afar and admired her great beauty. He made the decision at this time to acquire her for himself. He discussed the possibilities with his major-domo, Rakon. He proposed that if she would not come willingly, that the King could capture her and hold her forever. All that would be necessary would be to get her bodyguards out of the way, and since she was only a woman, they could trick her into special room designed to hold anyone indefinitely.

When she arrived, he permitted her an audience but determined that her bodyguards could not attend her in his presence. With great trepidation, she agreed since she felt that she needed a special boon from him and must trust his motives. When she arrived before him, she noted his intense stare, almost as if she were being examined as a prime animal. He had Rakon bring forth a chair so they could converse in comfort. It also allowed him to gaze upon her seated form. He was dark haired, with a small black goatee and was handsome in all aspects.

Sophia thought he might be a true companion for her, but then she noticed a certain hardness about the eyes, which when examined closely led to a seemingly calculating nature in his demeanor.

She burst right into her request, "I need a companion to share my life".

He gazed upon her beauty, and licked his lips. "I see" was all he said in return.

She could feel the sexual heat from him and she burst into rhapsody about all she had to offer, her fine outline, her friends among the beach animals, her caring and sweet spirit. She needed a soul mate which could share her thoughts and be an equal to her. The king had always ruled and was not looking for an equal to share his life.

As he stroked his short black beard, he thought about her comeliness and her need for a soul mate. No woman had ever refused his attentions, so he had grown callous about his approach to Sophia. He desired her greatly, but had no wish to woo her into his bed. He determined to use Rakon's plan and trick her into staying as his concubine in his mountain palaces.

Rather than offer her an immediate agreement, he told her "He needed to study this matter thoroughly and that he would give her an answer tomorrow."

He escorted her to rooms next to his and led her inside. The rooms were coldly beautiful, with views of both the southern forests, but also of his second palace just miles away. She could see it shining in the distance and as she walked out upon the balcony to see it without obtrusions, she heard a snick behind her. She turned quickly, but the king was nowhere to be found. She also saw that her door had no interior hardware and was magically protected so that she could not change into just a spirit form. She had effectively been trapped as surely as a swallow in a cage. Too late, she knew then that the

"Mountain King" could not be trusted.

She yelled through the door, but all she heard was laughter from the other side. He spoke through a small panel in the door, "I, too am lonely. If thou agree to become my wife and vow to stay with me in my mountains, I shall release you and pay you great honor. You shall be my queen."

Her answer was filled with scorn when she responded with "I knew I could not trust you, you are fickle as a weasel. I would miss my beloved realm and gradually wither away and die if I stayed with you. I refuse you and your offer. I also tell you that eventually your mountain palaces will be swallowed up by the sea."

His laughter echoed throughout the palace as he told her, "Then you will never leave my home until the sea comes to claim you"

However, her bodyguards were not idle during this time. They realized she was alone and at the mercy of this treacherous king. They too had been locked in a room without an exit, but their skills might be able to overcome the mountain king's guards, if they developed a plan. Raven had observed many telltale signs that the King was not honest and now their confinement merely confirmed his assessment. Their room had no windows or balcony, or Eagle and Raven would have escaped easily. The only way out was through the door without hardware.

As usual, the first to speak was Raven, who said, "I cannot believe that I fell for such an obvious trick."

Eagle pontificated "How can they treat ME this way." He always thought that he was beyond other animals or people. He always had the appearance of a major stick up his ass. He was obsessed with his own aspect and would do anything to avoid looking foolish.

Crab, not known for quick thinking said, "Hell, everybody treats me this way, I can practically hear the boiling water getting prepared, while they melt the butter."

Octopus who had turned stone gray to blend into the background walls said, "Enough! There must be a way for us to get out. We each have talents."

Raven thought and looked closely at the door. He could see that it was very solid, but it had a major gap at the bottom.

He asked Octopus, "Can you squeeze through the crack."

Octopus slid over and examined the crack. I can't get my beak through the crack, but I should be able to reach the lock by squeezing a tentacle through the crack."

Crab said, "If we can get the door opened, I can scurry along the walls until I find Sophia."

Raven thought long and hard about this plan, since he was the craftiest of all of them. Finally, he agreed that the attempt should be made.

As Octopus crept under the door, he quickly glanced down the hallway. One of his huge eyes peered through the crack and so that although a guard was present, he had drifted off to sleep. The guard never perceived that anyone could escape from that room. Octopus, oozed into the hallway and reached up with a tentacle and gently moved his tentacle into the door lock, he applied pressure to each tumbler until he heard them snick into place. As an added precaution he had changed the color of his tentacle to match the exact color of the door itself. He then released the door.

Crab told the others, "Remain here and I will return once I locate her room". burst out and climbed up the wall sideways and was rapidly out of sight near the ceiling. His legs ended in sharp spikes that he used to grip any imperfection in the castles surface. He was careful to go slow, so as not to create any kind of clacking noise that might alert the guards.

Octopus quickly closed the door behind him and the crab used every little imperfection in the walls to creep along jamming his eight legs into the slightest crevice. At each open doorway he would extend his eye stalks and peer around the corner, without exposing any of his shell to view. After exploring several hallways, he found a room with an open window and crept out and proceeded to look into each individual room from its balcony. Now he needed to find Sophia. He looked throughout the palace, creeping silently along the rafters until he finally located her sitting quietly sobbing on the floor to her room.

He whispered, "Fear not, my lady. We have a plan to rescue you."

Her sobs quickly changed to gentle laughter at seeing her friend, the Crab, waving its pincers in the air.

Crab told her "Maintain your stout heart and stand along the balcony and await your rescue." Before she could say anything, Crab had scurried back out the balcony and was gone.

Once back to their cell, Crab had octopus reopen the door and they all tumbled into the hallway. They were trying to make sure that they were as quiet as possible, so imagine a Raven and an Eagle tiptoeing through the hallways. Finally, they found a nearby empty room with a window. Raven told Crab to climb on his back, while the bigger octopus would reside on the Eagle and they flapped their way into the open sky. The guard awakened at the flapping of the wings and shouted the alarm.

The palace came alive with their pursuers trying to catch the four of them before they could reach the outer battlements. But they were fleet of wing, even with the weight on their backs. With crab yelling directions, they flew down and grabbed Sophia by the shoulders and then glided out over the palace and down the mountain. The "Mountain King" saw his plan being foiled, and in his rage at been spurned he laid a deathly curse upon her.

He shouted, "You will never find lasting peace, and you will feel the curse of mortality."

As she heard the "Mountain King" curse, initially she responded with tense laughter, but she worried what the curse meant. She was troubled as she and her bodyguards traveled back to her own realm.

As Raven and Eagle lightly placed her on the shore of her domain, she saw a young boy walking down the beach. As they watched the boy began to leap amongst her logs, He scared her bodyguards as he came and laugh at some inner game he was playing. along the logs and they scurried off to the depths of the Sound and trees. She looked into his spirit and saw that his soul was bathed with a silvery light. He had deep set gray eyes, tousled auburn hair, and a carefree manner. He was both old and pure but his demeanor naïve. She began to reach out to him with her spirit and gently touched his soul. She sensed that he might be both the companion and the ally she would need to defend herself from the "Mountain King".

The Importance of their Meetings

Now that the professor had told the story about Sophia and her escape, he needed to show how they met and how she had the impact she did on his life. He wrote that even as a young boy he had always been precocious, as well as sort of a geek. Forced to wear glasses from the age six onwards, he developed into a gawky, studious, and withdrawn child. He had learned to read and tell time when he was only three. With the support of his mother, he had learned phonetics and by the age of six was working on basic algebra. He worked his way through the Encyclopedia Britannica. He was careful to hide his rebellious nature at school, but was hardheaded about learning in general. He was obstinate (stubborn) when he thought he was right, but ethical in all his approaches to his fellow schoolmates.

Thus, in the summer of his fifth year, when Sophia first touched his life, Ray felt the first inklings of love. Although Sophia was much older and more experienced than he, she took on the appearance of a young girl in pigtails and overalls when she first met him. He gravitated to her and felt her soul when she touched him. They had such a common approach to life; it was probably inevitable that they would love one another. Initially, she was careful to maintain a certain distance in their ages, but later on she just adjusted to whatever his current age was at the time. Being wildly different in physical attributes, genders, and species; it is amazing that their love managed to transcend all those issues.

Ray had always been a lonely boy turned inward by the constant movement of his family. His father was a journeyman pipefitter and moved to wherever the work was. Never able to make friends fast or easily he turned inward and lived in fantasy worlds created by books and TV. Because he lived in a fantasy world, his soul was ancient and serious, with a desperate need for meaningfulness. His Mother had created a household where ideas thoughts and deeds mattered. His Father believed in hard work and perseverance and that they created the man. Ray became the intellectual son, the one who did his chores, did his schoolwork, but lived in the realm of monsters and demons.

His Mother and Father worried about him because he lived in those fantasy worlds which they could not see. He was not surly or curt, just withdrawn and preoccupied. His conversations were disconnected with their reality and he seemed inept socially. For years, Sophia's intense love did her best to comfort him when he was sad, play with him when he was mischievous, and listen to him when he just needed to talk. Their initial conversations were decidedly one- sided, not because she was silent, but because he had yet to learn her language and the gentleness of her thoughts. It was as quiet as a wind- blown sigh, but as he grew in age and understanding, her voice became clearer. When needed, she could be almost shouting at him with the answers to his concerns. And although to most of mankind she had the appearance of being cold and lifeless, to him she opened her heart and her secrets and showed how much she had hidden beneath her outermost shell. She was always friendly and polite with visitors, but she was always his Beach.

The Bodyguard's Counsel

Raven had thought long and hard about how Mountain King could affect them. The Mountain King hated not only Sophia and her bodyguards but any human being in general. He did his best to pour fire and ash down upon them whenever possible. Raven believed that as the number and impact of human beings manifested themselves in the area, they would need a champion to help people understand the dangers of the Mountains and the worthiness of Sophia and her beaches to provide a full quality of life.

Deciding to use his guile, the Mountain King sent his messenger, Rakon, to tell Sophia that they should reconcile. She thought deeply on this matter. Finally, she called her friends together once again to help her decide. Octopus and Crab sat close by the shoreline, while Eagle and Raven sat on tree limbs which overhung the water. As usual, crab was dragging the carcass of a small clam for a snack. While they awaited Sophia, he munched contentedly upon the flesh of the mollusk. Octopus looked over and hoped that crab was so preoccupied that he might be able to grab him. As he stretched forth his tentacle, he caressed the top of crab's shell.

Crab just as casually reached up with one pincer and grasped the tentacle and said, "Unless you want to be the first septopus, you will put your tentacle away."

Octopus quickly tucked all her tentacles under her mantle.

Finally, Sophia arrived, she told of the opportunity to meet with the mountain spirit, and how she felt that he might offer reconciliation. Raven looked dubious, but Crab, Octopus, and Eagle immediately offered their support.

Raven had been thinking about this situation for a long time. He fidgeted on the branch and lastly said, that he did not believe the Mountain King. He told of how he should not be trusted and how he had always been deceitful in the past. Finally, he convinced the others of his concerns and they all advised Sophia to wait and just avoid his offers.

With her refusal, the Mountain King pondered and plotted a

different tack to capture her. He resolved to work with the new humans that were arriving in the area. In contrast to the Native Americans, they had never seen his treachery. These new denizens were also greedy and easily twisted to achieve short term goals. They did not live with the land as much as change it to their purposes. He had seen how San Francisco Bay was once pristine, but had now been changed to a polluted waterway, choked with chemicals and the by-products of their industry.

Alone, with Her

Although, Sophia was the spirit of a beach only a mile and a half long. To Ray, she could be just a disembodied voice, or appear to be ready to play. Usually when Ray was alone, she materialized, but if he was with others, she would just talk quietly in his ear. Ray was gawky and skinny to the extreme, but with those eyes which pierced to your very soul. Sophia was always one of the most beautiful beings he had ever seen. She resided on a north to south stretch on the western edge of one of the most beautiful waterways in the world, Puget Sound. Standing anywhere with her, he could see Mount Baker in the North, the small communities north of Seattle, Seattle, and ending at Mount Rainier.

Her beach was covered in logs that had been laid on her shores during the heyday of lumbering the area. Huge log rafts used to ply their way along the shores from where they had been harvested on their way to the mills in Port Townsend or Port Gamble. When storms would catch these huge rafts in the open, the logs would bounce out of the rafts and be deposited along the beaches in the area. In particularly heavy storms, it might actually break the links in the rafts where the logs were chained together. Some of those logs had been deposited on her shores. You could tell them from the huge bore holes in the ends of the logs that had provided purchase for the chains that held them together. He would go down and just sit on the logs and wait. Sophia would appear quickly and they would sit and watch the waves beach themselves over and over. Eventually, Ray would ask her to tell him a story. During one of her first talks with him, she told him that the mountains housed her now mortal enemy. This was a story that he loved to hear over and over as he sat with her among the logs.

His First Break

Professor Durant looked up at the clock, and suddenly realized that it was now three in the morning. The effort of covering Sophia's initial story in a lecture had drained him both physically and emotionally. He closed his eyes to take a quick cat nap, determined to keep up with the story and tell all of the events which had made him the individual he was today. He decided to continue after that short nap. He traveled back to the time, when his entire world had been the beach, and his only concern was to step along the rocks and sands and watch his shadow grow with the day. Soon he was snoring quietly in the soft comfortable chair, with his feet crossed upon the desk.

Waking up eight hours later with a crick in his neck, he thought of seeing Marcie, his best friend and lover. They both were independent and single, but they had an agreement that if either of them needed the other, they would drop everything and make time available. If she needed him or he needed her, they only needed to use their code phrase of "Dalmation Coast", to get the other to come their aide. He called her cell phone and left the phrase on her voicemail.

Given his current overall weariness, he decided he needed some refreshment and perspective before he went any farther. To just go home and have dinner and relax before returning to the story of how Sophia changed him forever, was not enough. He required conversation and re-affirmation before he lost himself in the story again. As he got up and stretched and then went outside of the office, he found a typist waiting to help prepare his lecture series. She was a mousy creature that had never finished her degree work, but had dropped out to take a job. She had a perpetual downtrodden look about her, like life was just a burden to be survived. That the administration had assigned him this secretary/typist seemed a nice gesture but he realized that it was also a thinly disguised ruse to place a spy to tell them what his topics would be. She had already started working on the manuscript. Before he could leave, he got his coat. He found her standing at his threshold holding his work in her hands. She had a concerned look about her and then spoke of her concerns.

She said, "Professor, I think you should rethink your approach..."

He reacted with, "Why".

The secretary looked at the floor and then said, "It will tarnish your reputation, anger the Dean, and cause people to think you have lost your mind."

He studied her for a few moments, saw that her concern was truly her belief and then said, "I can see where you would have that opinion, but would you wait until I tell the full story before you make a judgment?"

"What will I tell the Dean when he asks me what you are working on?" she worried. "He expects me to keep him appraised and to give him what I type each day."

His original estimation being confirmed, that she was a spy and that the Dean had sent her to keep tabs on his progress, he said "Tell him, I am preparing lectures on the interrelationship between animals and humans; and that I am telling how my desire to become a teacher was first awakened." He suggested. "I will give you some of the more innocuous sections to give to him."

"The Dean says it's my butt on the line, so why should I lie to him?" she asked.

"When you were a student of mine, I remember you reading some romance novels: don't you want to find out the story of Sophia? He gently asked. "I can keep the innocuous pages here; in case the Dean comes by but I will hide the other pages at my home."

She brightened at the thought of a true romance story and thought for a long moment and finally said "Alright Professor, I will type up your story, but it better be as good as you say", was her response. He decided as he listened to her that the lectures could not just be about Sophia, but had to include all the things she had taught him, in her wisdom. He would intersperse her conversations, with the stories of his youth and what he discovered through the years concerning beach life, biology, geology, and human nature itself.

Sophia's Physical Attributes

As the spirit of the Beach, her home had enormous physical attributes which changed with the 16-foot tidal cycles in the "Sound". At high tide, the extreme north end was an old rock breakwater, where the water would lap up against this wall of rocks and would be impassable to most people. To the south was a huge sand bar, tidal pool, and ended in a kelp forest. She had developed a concave crescent which ran deeply into the land just before the bluff that led to his house.

Throughout most of his life, her midpoint was an old Navy dock which had been used to degauss ships prior to entering the mined passages to Bremerton Navy Yard. The dock also had a wooden piling breakwater providing wave protection. She then ran south into a huge half-moon crescent which came almost up against the 100-foot bluffs south of the dock. At low tide, the north breakwater jutted out into the bay for 200 yards, the area in front of Ray's house was a flat eel grass area extending out about 100 yards from the bluff, and south of the dock the area was a vast tidal pool extending out 300 yards with huge sand bars protecting the inner quiescent pool.

The beach had several areas of soft sand, and was covered with logs from the north breakwater to the dock. Sophia loved these logs since it gave her protection for erosion during the winter storms. Although at high tide, the beach seemed sterile and uninviting to marine life, the interface between the Beach and the Sound was filled with a huge host of marine life. There were thousands of sand fleas, barnacles, steamer clams, butter clams, horse clams, starfish, geoducks, gumboot chitons, tube worms, flounder, cutthroat trout, perch, rock cod, salmon, jellyfish, sea anemones, tube worms. sea slugs, sea cucumbers. moon snails, red rock crab, Dungeness crab, spider crabs, purple beach crabs, limpets, eel grass, sea weed, kelp, sea pens, dogfish, ratfish, ghost shrimp, sea lions, and sea otters. Thus, it was a treasure trove of new things for any curious child, and for him became an area of intense enjoyment and interest.

Sophia had contacted many human beings before but she threw herself into the effort of reaching the deepest parts of the boy's soul. Sophia also knew that although she could live much longer than the boy; her days were also numbered; both by the natural elements and potentially the "Mountain King's" curse. She felt in the deepest sense that she was balanced upon a precipice where the slightest misstep on her part would send her tumbling into the depths of the Sound. She had already seen her beach change radically with slumps and landslides.

She explained one day to Ray, how she had met her bodyguards for the first time. He was shocked and amazed, since he could still see the cedar hanging over the water, but the slide had been reclaimed by the elderberries and blackberries. From that point on he was extremely wary whenever he passed close to the cliffs south of the dock. He also decided to look into the geology of the area which created this unstable condition.

He said, "It is not enough to just love the young man, he needs to be the right person,

and we must take every opportunity to teach him how things interact and reach a balance."

Crab, for once without stuffed into his mouth, stepped forward and said "I will teach him that the death of a single organism is all part of the ring of life. That all beings on the beach are food for some other species, until the energy returns to the original species." The others looked at crab with new respect. They had always thought of the crab as a stomach with legs, but this was a very profound thought.

Octopus changed colors from blending into the beach to bright red and said, "I will teach the lad that not all knowledge and brains exist only in humans, but that other animals and body shapes contain the ability to think and plan.'

Stiff-necked Eagle usually seemed imperious and above it all, but he offered, "I will teach the boy patience and the skill of observation to learn how your dominion has developed into a strong and viable ecosystem.

Finally, they all looked to Raven, who spread his wings to encompass them all and after deep thought said, "I remain unconvinced that he is the best choice, but if he will listen, I will teach him the value of friendship and the need for loyalty to a common cause. Remember Sophia, it is not enough to just love the boy; we will need a champion to defend us in the near future. We need to teach him not only about you, but also how all of the beach creatures interact with each other."

Sophia thought of what Raven had said, and despite remembering the curse of the Mountain King, decided to use all of her efforts to reach out to the youth and entice him into her realm. She also told her bodyguards that her life depended upon the vitality of the beach. Her strength derived from the myriad forms of life and their interactions. Any loss of species or habitat would weaken her and if enough of the habitat was destroyed, she felt it would threaten her very life. She would need a champion among the humans to keep the beach healthy, and she thought this boy was the right choice to become that champion. She also knew he was also lonely and would spend hours just roaming along her shores. They decided that she would choose the right time to begin the teaching and Ray's real education would begin. He continued to go to formal school, but his love was the beach and what he learned from Sophie and her friends were the most important things in his life.

Everywhere he looked all along the beach, Ray could see slumps of earth and trees. Sophia told him that the geology of this area was built upon the effects of the last ice age, where glacial sheets moved down from Canada and scoured out the long chasms of both the Sound and Hood Canal. In between, was the Kitsap peninsula of which the beach was an integral part. That peninsula is essentially a glacial moraine which was deposited between the two arms of a much deeper glacier. As such it had a layer of blue clay overlaid by a sand/rock conglomerate. When layers of sand and gravel lie above less permeable silt and clay layers, groundwater can accumulate and zones of weakness can develop. In Puget Sound, this combination is common and widespread. Thus, whenever enough water flowed underneath this conglomerate above the relatively impervious clay layer it caused the movement of the conglomerate leading to a slump. This is what occurred when Sophia and her friends first met.

This slumping will eventually lead to the entire peninsula flowing into the Sound and will reconnect the two features of the Sound and Hood Canal. In fact, the front of his family's property above the beach had exactly this appearance. The microenvironments which held the diversity of organisms was also greatly due to the Navy's creation of the dock, which helped to develop homes for many organisms and was instrumental in the creation of the large sand bar and tidal pool.

Ray's father was always trying to find a simple way to reach the beach, as he disliked using the neighbor's stairs. First, he attempted to cut into the upper cliff a set of switch-backs, which would allow you to walk down the cliff to the lower slide area, where you could just walk down the remainder of the slump to reach the beach. In between was a veritable forest of blackberries. These were not the ordinary blackberry bushes, but had the appearance of the thickets of the forest of magical vines in Sleeping Beauty. Blackberries maintain a relatively unique capability to lean over and when the very top of the vine can reach the ground it will set down more roots. The vines on the boy's property reached well over 25 feet in length and were easily two to three inches in diameter.

Now, his father was not a mean man, he just liked to work. And he loved to have his children along to help him work. Ray's most common memory, growing up was spending weekends cutting and loading wood into the truck with his Dad; or chopping down blackberry vines with a machete. It would take them all day to knock down, remove and burn a 16-foot square of blackberries. Since this was within hailing distance from Sophia, he always found it hard to remain on task.

Many spring, summer, and fall weekends, Ray found himself praying for rain just to avoid the need to work all day on a weekend to remove blackberries. Unfortunately, despite the image created by the media, it rarely rained in the Northwest in sufficient quantities to dampen his Dad's enthusiasm for working on the blackberries. His father began bringing home 5 gallons of diesel fuel to assist in burning them out in great swaths. It was only later that they learned that blackberries loved to have the ground burnt from under them, since it removed all of their natural competitors. Each year, the blackberry patch grew bigger and wider, until it was like the myth of Sisyphus, a never-ending chore which never reached an end.

During his youth, his family was one of the few permanent residents of the area. It was not a bedroom community for the Seattle area, but was used primarily for summer vacations. In fact, the nearest person Ray's age was over 3 miles away in town. This probably contributed to his complete lack of social skills and quirky behavior. Each year his mom would ask him if he wanted to go to camp for the summer and each year his answer was an adamant "No!". He was never comfortable around girls and lacked social skills for chit chat common in his age groups. He was always thinking deep thoughts and delving into the mysteries of life and the world. He found most conversations with his peers to be mundane and colloquial.

Sophia used Ray's lack of social skills to offer to teach him the deeper mysteries of the beach. She would always challenge him with a new situation of condition and make him think of the ramifications of changing this situation. He became a lover of essay questions and story problems, where he could show off his skills of locating hidden meaning in the most commonplace events. She told him the story of her escape from the Mountain King. At first, he didn't believe it; but as he saw how distraught she was and that she was actually worried about the curse, he came to believe. He did his best to console her and make her realize that she had many friends among both the animals and humans. He told her that he would tell all his friends to get the widest amount of familiarity to the human population.

His family had a party telephone line which used only five numerals. They would listen for their individual rings, to answer a call meant for them. As a source of entertainment, this did not preclude other people from picking up their phone and listening in to whatever conversations were ongoing. This coupled with Lizbeth, the telephone exchange operator, who kept track of everyone made for a real community feeling.

For example:

Charley calls up the central exchange...

Hey Lizbeth, connect me with Bill Adams.

You know I would Charley, but Bill just left on the ferry. He said he was going into town to check on the new Buicks.

Did he say when he would get back?

No, but his wife is in Olympia taking care of her sick sister, and you know those two cows of his will raise holy hell if they aren't milked by six.

Yeah, I can practically hear them bellowing now; I'll try him around seven. Thanks, Lizbeth.

Be that as it may, no one ever called Ray, and thus he was relatively unaffected by these types of situations. It did mean that there was very little in the way of noise pollution. Anyone who truly listened could sense Sophia's spirit quite clearly. There were no car sounds, whistles, or other people noises. He could tell the time of the day, by hearing the freight train clearly across 20 miles of water, or the sound of the old steamer leaving or returning from the day's trip to Canada the sound of any major ship would resound in their ears long before it showed itself approaching Seattle or Tacoma.

As a common practice of the times, Ray had family chores to do, such as bringing in a wheelbarrow full of wood for the fireplace, stacking it in the garage, doing his homework and putting his stuff away. His usual method for putting stuff away was shoving it under the bed. As soon as he was done, he races off down the cliff to spend "quality time" with her. Initially, he had to have someone like his brother go down to the beach with him, but his brother become very sports oriented in Junior High school and was rarely home before six in the evening. Those were different times and his Mom allowed him to sally forth and explore the beach alone. Although his mom would periodically check on him, the isolation of the area and knowledge of his good sense permitted his independence. Nowadays, a little piece of glass seems to make a playground unusable, but he was constantly exposed to natural hazards such as waves, tides, rotten logs, sand fleas, etc. for most of his young life and grew to respect the dangers and opportunities given to him.

Sophia was always busy and relatively noisy. The hissing of her waves as they hit the shore, the sound of the beach rock grinding against each other adding their own crackle to the mix and overall, the calls of the seagulls as the glided over the beach and dock. And during the night, the frogs of the salt marsh chimed in with their chorus. When she was angry, the winds increased and the waves pounded on the shore like a bass drum. The movement of the rocks added even more to the noise level as they made the more subtle sounds of the snare drum. One day Sophia decided that Ray should do more than just play on her and began to teach him lessons. For his first lesson she had Ray lay on logs, while she told him to watch the Eagle.

Ray watched as Eagle coasted from the forest down to an old crag. He watched as hours went by and Eagle moved only her neck.

Sophia told Ray that the important thing was that the Eagle had been patient as she studied the surface, until he found the largest fish to take home and feed her children. Ray understood and remembered that lesson the rest of his life. He always tried to observe how the system worked prior to affecting the situation by his interaction. As Sophia's friend, he learned to hear those sounds and to listen to the more subtle undertones which were her real voice as she told all of her occupants that she was their guardian and not to worry. It was these conversations which grew into a deep and abiding love for each other.

Ray's Mom eventually learned that he needed time both alone with his imagination to build an understanding of his life. If it was stormy and raining, their family would watch their old black and white TV, which got two and a half channels or read their library of books. He varied between comic books or encyclopedias for most of his readings. This gave him both a sense of imagination and of history, as well as a love for the written word. But given even half way decent weather his choice was almost always to return to his love, the beach. There is something almost magical about any beach, where the activity along the shore is continual, but soothing. There is an old adage that you go to the mountains for stimulation and to the ocean for peace. With Sophia, he spent many hours just being with her and listening to her waves rush in and out. Each wave seemingly its own individual entity but also the same as all the previous waves. He was more at peace with her than anywhere else in the world. He could sit for hours on a single log, just watching the waves and tides and currents transforming the shoreline. The smells and the sounds were also unique, and he recognized the subtle shades of odors from her versus any other entity. Many people misunderstand the smells and classify it only as decay or the smell of the ocean, but it is not. It is a subtle combination of marine growth, salt, and wood.

Sophia confided in her comrades, that her feelings for the boy were deepening into a strong and abiding love. Crab, Octopus, and Eagle rejoiced in her changes as she grew more devoted to the boy. Raven was a little more judgmental and wanted to know where this would end up in the great scheme of their lives, since he also had seen many changes in both Sophia and the boy. He tried to state his concerns about their differences, but was rebuffed by Sophia's steadfast belief that her love would always carry the day.

As with any great love, the boy grew to know her, by her look, her sounds and even her scent. In much the way a woman and her perfume perform magic and create a mystery as they combine, Sophia had a unique scent. The overwhelming odor when you get to any ocean beach is salt. The salt is thrown into the air with each drop of water from a wave. But as he spent time with her, he began to smell the undercurrents of other odors.

The smell of cedar and fir trees along the beach, coupled with the smell of wild roses and rhododendrons. During the spring and summer, the smell of elderberries, blackberries and salmonberries combined with the odor of marine growth dying and decaying along the beach such as eel grass or kelp, along with the unique scent of barnacles and anemones losing fluid to the sun at low tides.

Everyone has heard the stories of how salmon can find their original birth streams to return to spawn, and in a similar fashion Sophia had her own unique odor. Anyone can sense when they are close to the ocean, but his recognition of Sophia went way beyond that ability. He could recognize her odor in the same way that you can smell a woman's perfume long after she has left a room. Sophia had the odor of both the living and the dying, the smell of salt, seaweed, sand, and organisms. Those organisms contained both the healthy and the dying. She would not smell the same without an undercurrent of death hanging deep in the background. This smell showcases that the beach is both a living organism but also contains predators which live on each other's flesh and life. Like the salmon, you could drop the boy off anywhere near our beach and he would know where he was, just by the scents and time of year. As he absorbed the odors of her being she asked him some questions. As usual, their conversation was very simple and direct.

Sophia started out, "What would you like to do today?" as her waves gently bent upon the shore.

He thought of the fun playing amongst the logs, or exploring the piling of the Navy dock, but finally he asked her to tell him the story of the Mountain King again.

Sophia responded with a laugh and said "You already know that one by heart. What is really troubling you?"

Ray decided he needed advice most of all: He asked "Can you help understand my Dad?"

As the wind gently moved the trees, he heard: "What's going on?"

Ray discovered new strength to suggest, "He never listens to me and never explains why he wants something, and when I don't do it right, he gets mad and yells at me and makes me feel bad."

She used the scrabble of beach rock to ask: "Do you think you are bad?"

He thought back to all of the times it had occurred and confessed, "Sometimes, I don't' listen and I purposely don't do things right away. I think this frustrates him.

Her voice rang clearly to his soul, "What can you do on your part to repair your side of the situation?

He thought again of how often he had let things fester and grow and said clearly, "I can try harder and work harder to be happy about doing the work.

Sophia's advice was great for Ray, but also to all children to understand how their own behavior affects the situations where they believe they have no control. It solidified his love in her role as his trusted advisor and confidante. His ability to talk to her about any subject grew with each passing day. They did not always discuss issues, but sometimes just explored the sheer joy of their relationship.

Ray would eventually visit beaches in Hawaii, Mexico, Florida, and hundreds of other places, but nothing could compare to the shear variety of things which could be observed with Sophia. She taught him to look deeply into the ecosystem itself to see the myriad forms of life in even a teaspoonful of beach. Many of those other beaches are attractive, but have the appearance of a sterile and touristy environment. Although those other beaches had many beautiful and colorful fish and sometimes a great variety of coral, they did not even come close to the variety and mass of marine growth which could be found on his beach. His beach felt like a living breathing entity which harbored thousands of marine plants and animals along its shore.

Part of this variety is due to the pristine nature of the Sound, but also due to the low temperature environment. When he waded into Sophia's light surf, the temperature of the water was almost always between 50 and 55 degrees. He could gradually become numb to its affects, but when he finally got out of the Sound; his legs felt like they had a thousand needles poking in them and were incredibly itchy when the blood returned to the surface. Also, her winds and currents and tidal conditions changed constantly.

Coupled with the fact that the Sound is a working waterway and had thousands of ships passing yearly along the shore, he needed to pay attention to what was going on in the beach/shore interface. Some of the ships produced enormous three-to-six-foot breakers when they reached the shore and they could easily knock you off their feet and carry the unsuspecting out to where 3-4 knot currents would sweep you into a dangerous hypothermic situation. He gradually learned about these conditions, but during his youth, he just stayed out of the water unless he had a partner to help him if he got in trouble. At high tide, Sophia appeared to be quite sterile and uninteresting. But even at this time, she was an endless source of interesting things to do. There were logs which suspended over the water and could be a challenge to crawl or climb over. His family and few neighbors had installed ropes in the trees at strategic locations to allow beachcombers to swing past those high points of water. But, as with most of the Sound, Sophia's tides were 12-15 feet cycles, which would expose thousands of square feet of land at low tide which would be covered with marine life both above and below the sand. This is where she came alive and was a source of amazement on just the incredible diversity on and volume of marine life which was beneath the surface of her waters 80% of the time. As Ray saw this transformation, he developed an insatiable curiosity in the sciences of Oceanography and Marine Biology. He hoped that he would always be able to keep her safe from the Mountain King and other entities that would destroy her.

A Well Needed Break

Professor Durant took rubbed his eyes and went out into the antechamber.

He looked at the typist as she said, "Okay. When do we get to the sex and good stuff, this all seems weird while also relatively tame and boring."

"Patience, Patience; we'll get to it." was his only response. "I need some inspiration," he stammered. "I will be at Marcie's house." And with that one comment he ambled off to his car.

He called Marcie as soon as he was in the car. He used their special code (The Dalmatian Cruise) to let her know that it was a matter of some urgency or need.

He asked, "Can I take you out to dinner, I have something I need to talk about with you."

She quickly responded, "I just finished making dinner, but as usual I made too much, just come by and we can discuss it at my place."

"Great, I'll be there in twenty minutes", he said with some no small amount of relief.

As he rang her doorbell, he anticipated seeing her again. She was a tall willowy brunette, who kept herself taut at 60 by eating right and working out a couple hours at a gym every couple of days. She had that look about her that said she was secure in herself and fully capable of handling most any situation. Her eyes were dark brown and seemed to smile knowingly whenever he was not getting to the central core of their discussion. When she opened the door, he gazed upon a mature beauty which seemed genuinely pleased to see him.

"Come on in, the halibut is just about cooked" was her greeting.

He sat down at the kitchen table to a Caesar salad and proceeded to devour it with relish.

He hadn't known how hungry he was until just now. She smiled and said "Save some of that energy for me."
His mumbled response through mouthfuls of lettuce and parmesan cheese was "Don't worry; I have a feeling that tonight my hunger is insatiable."

After a wonderful slice of halibut, a small piece of bread and some pinot grigio, he finally pushed himself away from the table. "Are you curious, about why I need you tonight?" Of course, but I know you will get around to it before too long..." she asked quizzically, while smiling at his reticence.

As he came around behind her and nuzzled her neck, he whispered "First I have another hunger, which I hope you can take care of..."

Even through her sweater, he could see that her nipples had hardened in anticipation. "Well, I don't know, I don't want to be known as some easy woman" she sighed contentedly as he massaged the nape of her neck.

"Trust me, nothing about making love to you is ever easy" he teased as he continued to nuzzle and rub her back with his strong hands.

"Oh God, you always known where my buttons are" she said as she turned to face him.

"Let's start pushing some of those buttons and later I have a story to tell you" He murmured and gently led her into the bedroom. They approached each other like the wild animals they were at the time. Although they gently removed each other's clothing, they approached their actual flesh as if dinner had not been enough to satisfy their needs.

Later, as they lay naked on the bed; the kidded each other about who should retrieve the covers that were strewn around the bedroom. She finally gave in realizing that he could have stared at her body for hours. After finding a new sheet, they both laid back and stared at the ceiling. She used her fingertips to gently trace a design in his still dark and curly chest hair.

He started, "Now, lay right back and you'll hear a tale, a tale of a "

She said, "Please don't tell me this is about Gilligan's Island or I will have to attack you again."

"No, I need to tell you about Sophia and what I plan to do in my new lecture series. I need your advice on how I should sneak this under the Dean's radar." he declared mischievously.

"You know I have never liked that rabbit faced little weasel, in every sense of the word.

Tell me about Sophia. I have always known that I came in a distant also ran to someone in your life, so Sophia must be my competition." she said with an edge to her voice.

Durant started into the long story of Sophia and how his life had been affected by her. Marcie listened intently as an understanding of many of the silences which had occurred between them became explained.

He finally ended the story, and asked what she thought. Marcie thought long and hard about many issues and finally said, "Continue to keep the story hidden until the very last minute. I also think that you should invite some major personages to your lectures. Maybe even a TV Show would like this story. Then, when ferret-face finally sees your lectures, it will have the proper weight and momentum to avoid disruption from him entirely. In fact, I would love to see his face as you conduct these lectures."

As they drifted off to sleep in each other's arms, Ray prayed that his nightly dream did not arrive. Asleep, he could not control the demons that he had awakened. He felt himself transported back to his first classroom lecture. He was standing on the side as himself now, watching his younger version struggling with a lecture on marine biology. He sensed in the back row, that Sophia stood up and tried to get his attention. His younger version ignored her, and she gradually faded into a ghostlike shape and then disappeared. He cried out her name as he felt himself returning down a long tunnel to his sleeping self. He awoke with Marcie's arms around him, while he continued to cry out for Sophia.

Marcie asked, "Are you alright, you were having a nightmare."

Ray said, "I dreamed that she tried to get my attention, but I ignored her. I felt as if I caused her to go away."

Throughout his story, Marcie had gotten frostier and frostier. It was obvious that she was troubled by some aspects of his story. Before when the subject of their relationship had come up, he had always subtly changed the subject. She had thought that it was the normal males reserve about discussing their feelings. Now, she knew better. She had thought long and hard after he had fallen asleep, but mow she spoke seriously, "I don't like being the second fiddle in any relationship. Before I thought, that I was competing with your ex-wife; but I cannot compete with the shadow of a goddess. I think you need to leave."

Looking hurt but also understanding her feelings, he rose and quickly dressed and kissed her cheek as he left. He tasted the saltiness of the tears on her cheek. She never saw the tears which were just welling up in his own eyes as he walked down the path to his car.

Love

Even when Ray was young it was always difficult for him to properly express, what Sophia and her love meant to him. He believed that Sophia loved him, and that she would be there whenever he had needed it most. As he was growing up, he grew more adventurous and explored under her waves and she showed how rich she was beneath the surface. It showed him an example of a true metaphor for people in general, not to be fooled by exterior placidness or beauty. It was important to look inside each person for qualities which were hidden. This may seem to be quite anthropomorphic, but he actually believed that he could touch Sophia's very heart and soul and that she recognized him as a specific human being with whom she enjoyed spending her time and energy.

At every major turning point in his life, Ray would come to her and just express his doubts or concerns. Every time she would answer him in the language of the waves, and a new path or opportunity would become clear to him. Many times, he had a particular crisis in his limited life which seemed to him, to be the end of his world. Not being promoted to the top level of little league, a girl who rejected him at school, or looking at changing career goals in college would drive him to the edge of despair. A long walk on the beach, as he listened to Sophia's waves as she consoled him, would dispel those concerns and her conversation would suggest ways of proceeding which he might not ever have considered. In these ways, Sophia was much older and wiser than he, and had seen much happen during her long life. She taught him that although specific events could be disturbing, he should take the long view and ride with life as a long-term journey.

Her mixed past with the US Navy

One day, Sophia told Ray that she needed to tell him about herself in greater detail. She started with her past relationships with the Navy personnel, which had been assigned to the dock and degaussing station. She wanted Ray to know, that although she flirted with the Navy guys, Ray was her one true love. She launched into the stories about the Navy and the guys assigned to her.

As is typical of many of the loves in our lives, Sophia came with an interesting and sometimes mottled past. Before his arrival, she had an ongoing relationship with about 35 US Navy sailors. Having a contingent of Navy personnel stationed in her center, allowed her to be both playful and fickle. With those who did not give her the respect she deserved, she could be a cold and harsh mistress. For example, she taught her young sailors the dangers of treating her lightly and how she could react if scorned. The Navy personnel and the dock were to demagnetize the ships prior to entering into the Bremerton Navy Shipyard. This meant a fast approach and a quick turnaround to get the ships underway for repairs. The dock was less than a half a football field in length, but at the end of the dock, the depth changed from tens of feet to over 600 feet in depth. The day that they brought in and parked a carrier at the end of the dock was amazing for Ray to observe. The carrier looked and was huge, and just dwarfed the dock. Parked only 100 feet from the shore it dominated his eyesight and was remarkable to see that close.

The boy was intrigued by the terms degaussing and the fact that all of the adults seemed to have a different view of what happened at the facility. When he was older and in college, he examined all the literature and found out why the structure was important and why it became obsolete for surface warships. During World War, II all sorts of mines were developed and used. A particularly deadly variety was the magnetic mine which was engineered by the German naval research into torpedo and mine fuses. Ships gradually become more magnetic by traveling through seawater. They successfully developed a murderous magnetic proximity fuse. The magnetic mine was based on the principle that when the residual magnetism of a ship distorted the local geomagnetic field of the sensor, it activated the mine's magnetic needle in the trigger.

One of the countermeasures was the installation of wiping stations which degaussed or demagnetized the ship's natural magnetic field. For years after WWII, ships had either to be degaussed by a shore based wiping stations. Thus, each ship had a unique magnetic signature which is the total result of the materials used to build the ship. Degaussing refers to this process of neutralizing the magnetic field around an object. The process can be applied to any magnetic material, but originated during World War II.

However, in the late fifties, a sailor developed a method to degauss the ships at sea, which eventually made the Navy Dock and facility obsolete. Personnel would still be assigned there throughout the fifties and early sixties, but they had absolutely nothing to do. Bored young sailors are a perilous group at best, and these had a significant additional problem, in which they were stationed in the boonies and far from any kind of night life or adult entertainments.

Since their duties were no longer required, the young men looked for anything else to do to occupy their time. One day, they found an old speedboat. It had a dilapidated cabin and was about sixteen feet long. Ray watched as they hauled it down the road through the Station, manhandled it onto the logs and proceeded to fix it up. There was an actual workshop on the beach which they used to help prepare this new speed demon of a boat for their use. They spent all fall, winter and spring, rebuilding the hull and refinishing the exterior paintwork. Finally, they were ready to launch the boat. They bought a new Scott 40 horse outboard motor so they would be able to power their way over to the Seattle. They had purchased the new engine and used so many hours of refurbishment, claiming they would make quick mail runs to the Seattle APO as their justification for the effort. They made runs to Seattle every day for the first week, and finally the weekend arrived. Now the true nature of their efforts became evident, they planned on using the boat to go on liberty in Seattle.

Now, throughout their preparations, Sophia and Ray watched their efforts with interest. She had a wealth of knowledge about boats and seamanship. By and large, she thought that the navy guys were doomed to failure. Not because they didn't work hard, but they did not understand the inherent dangers of being on the water and the details of operating a small craft.

As with most young men, they were both overconfident and immature about life on the water. And, Sophia as one of the first feminists; had a mischievous side which loved to teach such young men lessons about life. She used her considerable powers to implant an image of herself in each young man. The image was of a younger woman with significant endowments, loose morals, and fun-loving persona. Not far from the actual truth. As they took the boat for its' first test run, they began to imagine the possibilities of meeting up with such a woman on their shore leave. When they returned to the dock, each of them was in such a hurry to change into their dress uniforms, which they assigned the retention of the boat to the newest and least knowledgeable of their colleagues. He tied the aft line to cross beam and the fore line to another.

As they went back to the barracks to get ready for a night on the town, the tide came in and the boat, not being tied by slip lines but by static ones, began to be pulled down by the ropes holding it to the cross beams, while the tide continued to put a strain on the hull. When the tide got high enough that the boat took water over the sides. The gurgling sound it made was interspersed with Sophia's giggles, as she fought to keep from laughing out loud at the mess she had made of their project.

Overall, this was an abject lesson concerning tidal cycles for young seamen, who were primarily from Iowa, Nebraska, and Oklahoma. The next few weeks for the Navy personnel were spent refloating, cleaning the boat and working the engine over completely in the shop at the station. Once again, the great moment came again, and they pushed off from the beach, started the engine and roared off to a grand Seattle evening. They did not wait for their most experienced member, the chief, since they didn't want any older guy holding back their fun in the big city.

Once again, Sophia gave her image of loose availability to those assigned to the boat. They pushed the boat into the surf, started the motor, without checking on the levels of gas. When they were just 150- 200 feet from the dock, the engine quit. It was then that they realized their second grievous error; they had failed to return the drain plug into the hull. Without the engine, that hole was now rapidly filling the boat with water. Despite all of their efforts to stuff it with their shirts, hats and other paraphernalia, the boat sank from underneath them.

Their frantic calls for help elicited laughter from their colleagues who they had left behind. But eventually a line was thrown to them to the boat did not make it and sank in haul each person back to the dock. approximately 300 feet of water, never to return. Sophia's chortles of laughter mixed with the outright guffaws of their fellow Navy men. Most of time, Sophia tolerated them and got along with their gullibility. But she shared with Ray that they were really not worth much of her time, since they usually were so geared to their comrades that they never really heard or understood her.

While the dock was active, there was supposed to be a 300-foot exclusion zone on either side of the dock, where civilians could not proceed. The facility had been almost decommissioned when he arrived in the area. Luckily for Ray, most of the sailors were bored and he could talk them into letting him dig clams and then returning the catch in the afternoon. And most of the time, unless a ship was in, they didn't care, so he could walk underneath the dock to get to the other side without any hassles. But not all of the Navy personnel were indifferent to her charms.

One day as the boy slipped surreptitiously under the pier, he heard a voice, asking him "Where do you think you are you going?" He was shocked one day to see a lone sailor sitting on the rocks and just staring out along the beach. Noticing the sailor's wide soulful eyes, he trusted him immediately. He covered his shock by lying that he was just going to get a couple of the purple shore crabs which lived under the rocks.

The sailor responded with "I have seen you many times on the dock and roaming the beach, what do you enjoy most about this place?" The young sailor seemed to really care about the boy's reasons, so he decided to respond with the truth.

He said "She and I talk and we play games". "She!"

The sailor asked, "Why do you say she?"

Ray replied, "Because she is a beautiful girl and I have seen her and spoken with her."

The young sailor said "She speaks to me too, but I have never seen her. I get ribbed all the time

by the other guys in the barracks, so I try and get away to just talk with her when I can. I love the feeling of her soul and her unbreakable faith in life".

Before the conversation could continue, Ray heard the other sailors yelling, "Come on weirdo, get in the jeep we are going back to the barracks."

The young sailor looked remorseful, but he eventually got up and climbed into one of the jeeps. Within the month, all of the Navy personnel had been transferred off the site and the young boy, never saw that sailor again.

Being only seven at the time when this occurred, the boy was convinced that Sophia had sent them away in order to spend more time with him. Opening up the area of both the exclusion zone and the dock, also meant that he had a huge new opportunity to spend quality time exploring all her many riches. The Navy sent the station and the dock into caretaker status. So even after the sailors left, one Civil Servant was assigned to keep the grass mowed and the building structures in shape in case they ever needed to return. Even though the youth was convinced that the whole beach was open to exploration, he was cautious and circumspect around the degaussing station and was always on the lookout for someone to chase him away from the area. But the caretaker was a nice man, who enjoyed the quiet life, out in the boonies. He lived in a small cottage with his wife above the main building for the next twenty years and the youth got to know him quite well. The caretaker was quite the lover of animals and developed a menagerie which used the fenced premises as a private little park. Ray loved the deer, raccoons and squirrels which regularly showed up for hand feeding.

Once, the caretaker even gave the boy and his brother, a tour of the facility. They marveled at the gigantic old growth beams which created the main living area. It had been built when old growth timber was readily available. The barracks spaces even had two pool tables and other entertainment available. The top of their personal tour, was visiting the light at the very top of the building. It was the youth's first exposure to physics of light, when they saw the Fresnel lens which he kept polished as a glittering eye on the world.

Once the Navy presence was gone, it still left the old dock as a resource for everyone to use. It was dilapidated, rotten in places, and generally would never be "allowed" in today's litigious environment. The piling hosted many different organisms, from fish to barnacles to anemones. The most destructive could not even be seen. The pilling had been infested with ship worms. The larva of these worms bored channels throughout the wood, eventually leaving only a shell of a structure which could be damaged by any significant contact. In the picture above, you can see that the worms had already caused the loss of some of the support pilings. Although it was posted with one small warning sign, because some of the pilings were gone and the dock had several big holes in the decking; Sophia and Ray conspired to use it to its full advantage.

Looking down through the holes in the decking he could observe hundreds of fish-eating marine growths from the piling. Although these were Sea Perch and very bony to eat, he still loved the fun of catching them and then releasing them back to the bay.

He looked for the perfect bait to use and as usual his beach supplied a wealth of choices. Clams would work, but were not available at high tide. Barnacles did not seem to appeal to the perch.

Although many people swore by the use of tube worms, he found which they did not attract these perch and were difficult to obtain at high tides. He then stumbled upon the perfect bait. This bait was always available, could be kept alive in a milk carton and were fun to catch. These were the small purple shore crabs which he found hiding underneath the big rocks at the high intertidal zone, but he knew that these were relatives of one of Sophia's friends. He decided he needed to ask for permission in this case.

One day, as they walked along the beach together, he asked. "Would crab mind if I used some of those small crabs as bait.

Sophia thought for a long time and then said. "I don't think he minds, since I have seen him eat them himself, but I guess I should ask." She was extremely proud at how the beach was working. How each organism was in balance with the others and she didn't want anything to upset that delicate equilibrium.

When she asked crab, he said, "The boy can gather any of my people he wants. I have warned them to stay out of the shallows, and if can get them with his hands, he's just getting rid of the stupid ones anyway. All I ask is that he doesn't use the traps like other people to capture and eat my kind. We are such hungry race, trapping us in a pot by luring us with food is just not fair. If he can catch them with his hands, it is a fair fight."

Sophia told Ray and made sure he understood the restrictions. He never used pots when he went looking for crabs but always just grabbed them with his hands. Also, in deference to his friend's friend, he never ate any of the crabs, but always gave them away to others.

For fishing equipment, his father was not about to allow Ray or is brother to use any of his salmon poles, so he bought them some hand-lines to use for fishing. The line was actually a thick twine, but the perch did not seem to care. Ray took and impaled the crab on the hook and then dropped it down in front of the perch. The fish would gobble it down, and then start circling faster and faster trying to wrap their line around a piling to break it. The boy became very adept and hauling up these fish, and then letting them go again to start the process all over again. He could fish for hours and never tire of the game. The perch didn't seem to mind overly much, since they were getting crab all day long and after a short battle were returned to the water to be caught over and over again. He learned, after hours concentrating on positioning the bait and waiting for the perch to take it, that tidal conditions were important to the fish feeding cycles. In between catches, he listened to Sophia as she murmured to him through the waves striking the shore.

In addition to the perch, the dock harbored thousands of barnacles, sea anemones, starfish, spider crabs, and tube worms. Looking down through the hole in the dock, it was like looking into an enchanted forest of life. The colors and variety of anemones present rivaled the finest aquariums in the world. Their flower like heads shifting back and forth in the currents and waves, harvesting what he later learned were plankton and small fish. The perch swam amongst them with seeming impunity, being too big to swallow. You could even see the occasional dogfish sharks swim through the area. The perch would scatter and hide when it approached and hide in the wing-walls of the dock and then return when it had moved on to deeper water. By looking through the hole in the dock, he avoided the shimmering effect of the sunshine and could easily see 15 feet or more below the surface. Being a lover of all animals, he would spend hours with Sophia, lying on the dock and just watching the parade of fish and other creatures beneath the pier. Seeing all of the fish and marine growth piqued his curiosity about what else was harbored by his love and she led him to the secret places where even more exotic organisms had established. These explorations led to his love of marine biology and had a great effect on his life.

These were different and more naïve times and as the boy grew older, he marveled that any government agency would ever allow the use of such a dilapidated and unmaintained structure. Given the nature of his current society, any danger would have to be precluded by a locked fence and severe punishments if someone used the dock at all. But in those days, he had cousins and school friends all over that dock, exploring and fishing and generally enjoying the resource. As long as they didn't cause any further damage or abuse the use of the dock, no one seemed to care.

It was also home to one of the prettiest occupants of the beach, seagulls. Seagulls had learned to propagate using the harder to reach areas of the dock to nest and raise their young. There calls were part of growing up along the beach, and it was part of the culture of Sophia to allow these birds to rest in her arms. In fact, when Ray reached puberty and his voice began to change, he could imitate the sea gull's calls with uncanny accuracy. The Sound at that time was full of herring balls, and thousands of stretches of beach where these seagulls could find food. The herring balls were an easy way to locate salmon, since the salmon formed the balls by preying on the bottom of the herring schools. The seagulls would mark the spot by diving into the top of the balls and getting their share.

Boris

When Ray was twelve, the Vietnam War was in full sway and his brother had unwisely lost his student deferment. His brother decided that his options were to join the services or be drafted into the Army, so his brother volunteered to enter the Air Force. Having rated as one of the highest candidates ever in mechanical repair, he thought he would be assigned to maintain aircraft somewhere in Vietnam. He was looking forward to working on the sophisticated engines employed by the air force.

However, just before he entered the service, his brother decided he wanted a dog. He brought home a 6-week-old Labrador/Samoyed puppy. Ray's mom was beside herself, in which she did not want a dog, but knew that the family would be stuck with the care and upbringing of a brand-new puppy. His brother took off for basic training. After six weeks he was sent off to the Strategic Air Command base in North Dakota. When he arrived, the only question which he was asked was "Can you type?" He spent his entire tour of duty performing clerical duties and never reached Vietnam. Back at home the puppy decided to chew everything in sight, including Ray's moms newly refurbished oak table. Given his penchant for chewing it is amazing that he survived his early childhood.

Ray and his dad inherited the raising of the Labrador puppy, who Ray promptly named Boris. Unfortunately for the Labrador, one of the few permanent families in the neighborhood, had a huge white Samoyed, and they had sold all of her puppies. She took over care of Boris. Ray and Boris would go down to the beach and the Samoyed would tag along. Whenever Boris neared the waves, the Samoyed would stand between him and the water. As Boris grew into a 110-pound monster, Ray's family had the only Labrador which was afraid of the water.

This did not stop Boris and Sophia from loving each other. Ray always imagined them walking on the beach together, when he was at school. Boris would patiently walk alongside of her and look up at her attentively, while she would show him how to find clams or crabs for his enjoyment. He had a huge heart and was just like a new born baby for Sophia. So, once he understood that clams were buried in the rocks, he would dig them up by himself and crunch their shells between his huge teeth.

Sophia took great pleasure in this and thought that a dog which would dig up and eat clams was humorous. His paws were always scarred deeply by the rocks and barnacles, but he continued to dig them up and eat them like hotcakes. Sophia took great delight in showing Boris all of the good things to eat and enjoyed his attentions and overall egalitarian tastes. He would try almost anything, but his greatest loves were the clams he could dig up and crunch, until the soft inner filling was available for swallowing. He was the only dog which constantly smelled of clams, the only thing missing was the garlic butter.

However, Raven took an instant dislike to Boris. He sent his brethren to torture him. They would never actually attack him, but they would tease him in his yard, by lazily flying back and forth across the front of the yard and get him to chase them. Boris would gallop from one side to the next and not notice that each trip brought him close to the high bank. Finally, the Raven would lazily cruise out over the bluff. Boris would try and apply the brakes and just land in the blackberries at the very top of the bluff. He never seemed to understand what they were doing.

Of course, this is the same dog which would ride in Ray's dad's 1955 dodge pickup, and sit up on the seat. He never seemed to understand that when the brakes were applied, he would go forward. Ray always remembered that was Boris' usual position after a stop which was his hind quarters on the seat, his chin on the dashboard and all four legs dangling in open air.

One day, Ray's mom decided that a Labrador which wouldn't swim was an embarrassment to the family. She and Ray loaded Boris into their dinghy and rowed a short distance away from shore. His mom said "Throw him in!" Ray probably weighed about 80 pounds and Boris outweighed him by at least 30-40 pounds. As Ray tried to wrestle him over the side, Boris wrapped all four feet around Ray and would not let go. The dog was as strong as a bear, and he DIDN'T want anything to do with that cold, cold water. Ray's mom came to the front to try and peel those legs off. Finally, both Ray and his mom went over the side, only to see Boris victoriously standing on the bow of the boat, still dry.

But Boris was a creature of his environment. He could run the beach for hours and loved to chase sea gulls and visit people and generally make a great big fool of himself to the enjoyment of everyone along the beach. One day, Ray's dad gave a neighbor a ride from the ferry dock after work. He was going to drop him at his house, but the man said, "No, I'll just run through the woods, it's only a couple of yards away". Ray's dad thought he would give him a break and turn on the outside floodlights to allow him to see his way. Unfortunately, he also let Boris loose at the same time. As the next-door neighbor loped through the woods, an enormous leaping shadow loomed up behind him. The neighbor let out a yelp and turned a hard right further into the woods. Boris, thought great, "We're going to play in the woods". Finally, Boris caught up with him and the neighbor realized that it was not some strange creature, just our dog and sheepishly walked home. Boris' usual position at home was laying full length on his back with all four legs spread to the corners of the family picnic table, enjoying the warm sun. He loved to chase things through the woods or race down the beach. At one fourth of July party, Ray had overheard the neighbor say that if ever saw a dog chasing a deer, he would shoot the dog. Ray's Mom jumped to the attack, to say both creatures were just following instincts, but the dog had a family somewhere which loved him. The neighbor took it silently, but Ray saw that he was unconvinced. One day, Ray couldn't find Boris, who was normally waiting patiently for him to return from school. Finally, Boris came home with three bullet holes in his side. Ray was sure that a neighbor had shot Boris, though he could not prove it. He had been shot by someone in the lungs and stomach, but had still managed to get home. Although they called the vet, nothing could be done for him. They buried him in the woods, within sight of his beloved beach. Sophia came and visited the gravesite, which was far from her domain, but it was to honor her pal. Ray heard her cry for the first time as she mourned the loss of a dear friend and companion.

It was at this point, that Raven came to speak to Ray privately. Raven told him, "I was watching your reactions about your dog. I have always been concerned about your seeming lack of emotion. When we need you to step forward and do battle against the Mountain King, you must use everything, including your emotions to defeat him or his minions. If you don't, he will win, because he is enormously powerful and cunning."

Ray replied, "I am not comfortable sharing my feelings with anyone, least of all during a battle of wills."

Raven scolded him, "I will speak to Sophia, but I am telling you now, YOU will need to use every capability you have to defeat the Mountain King." And then he flew off.

The Intertidal Zone

Ray never told Sophia of his confrontation with Raven, he just went back to his lessons and rededicated himself to learning about the Beach and the marine growth there. Sophia had daily tidal cycles of about 15 feet. She swung from the high tide levels to the extreme low tides, every twelve hours. The boy marveled at how far out the water could go and the acreage of marine growth which became apparent. From the shore at high tide, he couldn't see the numbers of animals per square foot which are in the intertidal zones. Fishing from the dock, he caught glimpses of the huge amounts of growth just under the surface. Turning over rocks and finding the purple shore crabs, Sophia began to lure him into a deeper relationship with her as a friend and confidant. She led him further and further afar to see the huge sandbar, the tidal pools, the eel grass flats and the kelp forest. In many ways it was like seeing a beautiful woman and being attracted to her; and then when you talk to her; discovering that they had much in common and she was actually a deeply soulful and loving companion. She would give Ray just enough observation of some unusual sea creature, which he felt he had to find out more about how each creature lived, what it ate, and what ate it. He found out that at that time, very little solid information existed concerning the interaction of all these creatures and he vowed to make it his life's work to remedy the situation as much as he could.

Walking directly out from the beach in front of his house, he walked over a seemingly sterile rock bed, covered with small round stones and old clam shells. At low tide, another twenty feet brought you to the beds of steamer clams and anemones growing in the rock/sand environment. These are the ones served as appetizers, when you order a bucket of clams in garlic/butter sauce.

A little further out brought you to a sandy stretch which was full of butter and horse clams. The last stretch before the low tide line was a small sand bar, covered with eel grass where crabs and flounders made their homes. Further out under the water, you could perceive that the marine growth continued to the geoduck beds, and where salmon and cutthroat trout would occasionally swim through the area.

His love for Sophia grew in intensity, with each new discovery. He explored each part of his love with additional focus and clarity as he grew up.

His initial stage was to look at these enormous growth systems as both a playground and source of food. He was never a great lover of the seafood he gathered, since it seemed like it was part of Sophia.

She counseled him and told him that she loved to furnish her treasures. She knew he appreciated them and thoroughly enjoyed catching them. She said that she grew more food on a constant basis. So, he learned, how to spot steamer clams from the telltale but minute holes left in the sandy surfaces; to tell the difference between a horse clam, good for only chowder, and a bed of butter clams; and finally how to wade out and locate Dungeness and Red Rock crab in the eel grass and pick them up with his bare hands without getting pinched. A necessary skill, since they could break a small stick with their claws.

Ray's father was a "journeyman" pipefitter so they went to where the work was. When Ray had first met Sophia, his family traveled almost every weekend from Pullman where his Dad worked; to Kingston, to work on their house. He hated these trips since they were almost 400 miles, and he usually became very carsick. By the mountain passes, his stomach had usually had enough driving, and they would finally pull to the side of the road so he could throw up. That still left a couple of hours to travel, so he would try and sleep the rest of the way.

One weekend, his family had taken a break from the house, and went clam digging. He decided that he wanted to show his classmates back in Pullman, the diversity of marine growth from his beach. His Mom allowed him to pick and choose some clams, shells, snails, and starfish and put them in a burlap sack to take to school for "Show and Tell". They kept them cool all the way home, by keeping them on ice in the trunk of the car. Monday morning rolled around and he took the burlap bag to school. On Wednesday, his Mom got a call from the teacher. She said there was an unusual stench coming from his desk.

His Mom asked him, "How did "Show & Tell' go."

Responding quickly, he said. "I showed some of my friends the stuff, but 'Show & Tell' is not until Thursday."

"Oh, my God", was all his mom could sputter out.

The next day, she took him to school and together they disposed of the stinking mass of marine growth, cleaned out his desk and spent the morning apologizing to the teacher.

Summer Visits with Family/Friends

Ray's parents came from the generation which had survived the depression, and they had had many brothers and sisters on each side. His father and mother each had two brothers and two sisters. Each of those families had between two to seven children each. Thus, there were a lot of cousins. They were scattered throughout the west, from Washington to as far away as Colorado. Many of these cousins came from city backgrounds and were used to city amusements for entertainment. Thus, the city cousins were kind of prissy and thought that the beach was not much fun, when compared to a mall or other city attractions. They would come to Ray's house and just mope around complaining about the TV or lack of shopping, etc.

Ray strived to show them how wonderful the beach was, but seemed to always receive the same response, that of bored and jaded children. They could care less about the games which could be made up and the rules of the beach concerning how to use her charms. They were usually very destructive with the environments, and did not care that the boy wanted them to see the beach as a friend and fellow playmate. Luckily there were a few country cousins which understood about nature and the fun which could be made with just simple pleasures of hide and seek or catching/releasing the fish around the dock. They were just as adventurous as he and his brother, and enjoyed the beach as much as they did. His country cousin's Mom and his Mom were sisters and best friends, and so they spent a lot of summers together. These cousins loved to fish from the dock, dig clams, wade in the water, and explore the beach.

But being located in a beautiful location, with excess space in his basement, his family had regular visits from both the city and country cousins or friends throughout the summers. Sophia always acted like a proper and good hostess for each group, but she also seemed to be glad when the hubbub subsided and it was just the she and the boy again. It was if at the end of the party, they would nestle in each other's spirits and talk about what had happened during their visits. They were just happier alone together.

As much as the country cousins enjoyed each other, there were dissensions even amongst themselves. In this group there was a middle child which did not pair up with the older or younger cousins. As an example, one day, the older two cousins were on the beach and she went to the bluff above them and yelled that their parents wanted them. After hiking up the beach up to the bluff and walking all the way back home, they arrived breathless to ask what was needed. They found out that their parents were playing pinochle and drinking, and said they hadn't wanted them at all.

Now the middle child, of course, had disappeared. They looked for her for a half an hour to apply a little retribution, but finally they gave up and went back down to the beach. Two hours later, dinner was ready and their parents sent her to get the two older boys off the beach. She went back to the same place on the bluff and yelled out to them, "that they were wanted back at the house". Like the little boy crying wolf, she wasn't believed. Unfortunately for the two older boys, they caught hell when their parents had to interrupt dinner and go get them to come back.

The biggest family event ever was in conjunction with the 1962 Seattle World's Fair. This was when the Space Needle was built and the boy had 26 people stay at his house at various times to allow them quick access to the Fair. There were more cousins, Aunts, Uncles, Grandparents, friends, etc. staying with them, where they all had to give up their beds and sleep in the basement. Everyone went to the fair and at some point, in time, but they also spent a week at the house, fishing, digging clams, catching crab, drinking and eating. The majority of the group was Scandinavian, which meant that the evening pursuits meant drinking and playing cards until late in the night.

Ray became concerned with the sheer number of animals which were being caught and eaten by his family.

He went down by himself early one morning and spoke to Sophia. "Sophia, is my family taking too many of your resources?" She responded with, "Look around you, how many old empty shells due you see? Do you see the carapaces of dead crabs, fish carcasses, and other animals? Your family is but a single miniscule entity enjoying just a small portion of my life. Let me have crab come and talk with you.

He had observed the eagle, but never knew which crabs could talk. When he realized that this was a special crab, full of magical presence, he relaxed a little. Crab spoke elegantly about the circle of life on the beach. He showed Ray how a flounder had attacked his relative, bitten off the legs to immobilize it, and then proceeded to peck away at the carapace until it breached its armor. The flounder ate the insides. He then showed Ray a crab which had caught a young flounder in its claws and was slowly eating the fish one bite at a time. Crab said look to the relationships amongst the animals on the beach. Starfish eat clams, but you do not always see how the clams filter out small Starfish larvae from the water and devour them in great masses. It is only when one group begins to dominate a beach and destroy that balance, where you should begin to worry. And then Crab retreated back into the depths."

Ray thought about this for many years and saw the wisdom of Sophia in how these interactions were balanced to maintain a healthy environment for all creatures. Ray quit worrying about it and enjoyed his cousins and the joy he saw when they enjoyed Sophia's charms.

Every night there would be some sort of party for the adults, while the kids played in the basement. Since there were over 15 kids, monopoly or other board games were out of the question. So, they created a brand-new game, unique to the basement. It had old tables, chairs mattresses, a furnace and multiple rooms in which to hide. One kid was designated "IT" and given a flashlight. He had to stay at the landing of the stairs and shine the flashlight around the basement looking for people. All the kids hiding were required to have some body part visible from the landing. The person being "IT" not only had to locate the person, but name them as well. If somebody was the first one caught and identified, they became "IT" for the next round. Occasionally, the parents would check on them, but they were usually drinking and playing cards upstairs and as long as the kids didn't start any fires and no one was crying they let them play until late into the night.

For beach adventures, Ray and is brother were usually running the fishing from the dock. This meant helping people get bait, bait the hooks, portioning out the landlines and helping generally with the efforts. His brother was in charge of the older kids and would lead them off on adventures along the shore. One afternoon, his brother led about six of the oldest along the beach, just as the tide was coming in, and the weather started to pick up. Realizing that the tide was going to swamp the beach where they had just been, he led everyone north around the rocks and then planned to go up the cliff away from the beach and get on the road to head home. They were never in any danger, and so they took their time coming home and explored some fishing shacks at the north rocks.

One of the uncles was worried about his kids and the rest of the group. It was now getting dark, and the winds and rains had come in with the tides. He went to the bluff and tried to shout for the kids, but rapidly realized that no one could possibly hear him over the storm. He went back to the house and tried to get the rest of the uncles to help him launch a search party. Possibly because he had been aboard the USS Helena, when it was sunk off of Guadalcanal, he took any sea water very seriously. He fretted and walked around like a caged animal looking for something to do. He repeatedly tried to organize a search and rescue party, but the family looked outside, and said they didn't think so. They told him that the kids are fine and will be back soon, so relax. Ray even tried to tell him that there were many ways off the beach and that he was sure they were all right, but the uncle ignored him along with the rest of the relatives.

Ray knew that Sophia would use this to have some fun. The Uncle could not let it go. He determined to walk the beach and search for them himself. He dressed in a parka and raincoat and took two flashlights. Down on the beach, he tried to go where he was sure the kids had gone.

Sophia told Ray, that she had to teach his uncle a lesson. Ray begged her to let it go, since this was one of his favorite Uncles. Sophia said, I cannot, such pride and arrogance is too much for me to leave alone. The Uncle saw that the tide had really risen. Sophia used her logs to entice him into a way to continue; if he could just leap over a log and swing under an overhanging limb. Just as he started, she increased the storm's power and allowed a large wave to sweep him away from the limb. Ray could hear her giggling as she saw him lose his balance and topple into the bay.

He fell in and found that the temperature of the Sound was not like the water around Guadalcanal. Not only was he sopping wet, but was also rapidly becoming hypothermic. He returned to the house just as the boy's brother was leading the missing troop of cousins down the driveway. The Uncle looked at him and didn't say a thing, but just went inside stripped of the wet clothes and washed off both the salt water and humiliation. It just illustrates that the beach would tolerate only so much from adults. She would allow some harvesting from the wealth along her shores, but she resisted their efforts to reach a deeper understanding of her. And she did her best to humiliate adults who had only a surface knowledge of her issues and dangers.

Perhaps his favorite memory with just the cousins is when all of the country cousins were exploring the tide pool south of the dock. There was always a period of adjustment when both sides met each other. Awkwardly, Ray would suggest that they go down to the beach. Usually, everyone piled onto the idea, and the five of them would troop off to the beach. Once down on the beach, they would think up games to play.

Ray would start with hide and seek among the piles of logs. But then one day his brother and older cousin decided to scare the heck out of them. To get rid of the little cousins, his brother told them to watch out for poisonous water moccasins since they would come out of the salt water march and sunbathe on the logs. They could never convince the younger ones to play hide and seek again.

As the tide retreated and exposed the sandbar, they would all troop off to look for clams, crabs, and other interesting stuff. Sophia had an enormous sand bar at low tide which encircled almost 2 acres of tide-pool.

As they were all walking along the sand bar, an enormous shadow of a fish swam through the embedded eel grass. The older cousins decided that as "great" hunters, they would find a weapon and land this beast. They went up into the logs and found a flat plank, which could be broken lengthwise and made into a sharply pointed board and waded out into the lagoon. As one cousin acted as the "Beater", Ray's brother held the spear ready to strike. Unfortunately for both of them, as the fish swam by, his brother threw the spear and hit the great fish in the head.

Now anyone can tell that hitting a fish of any type in the head with a piece of wood is going to do nothing except make the fish mad. The makeshift spear managed to penetrate the skin, but glanced off the hard skull underneath. Caught in a loop of skin, the spear began to gyrate rapidly as Ray's brother tried to hold on to it. It thrashed in his brother's hand, and as the wood began to twist in his hands, the great fish swam around his legs. It was a Ling Cod and probably weighed between 60 and 80 pounds. It continued twisting and turning, until it brushed up against the brother's leg. He let out a scream and was back on the sand bar in seconds. All of the cousins were laughing so hard, it took him many minutes to regain his composure. They never attempted to spear a fish again. When they told their parents, all they could do was laugh at the image of him trying to hold onto the stick with an 80-pound monster trying to yank free from the spear.

Once again, Sophia had used her wiles to teach everyone an abject lesson concerning the fish around her and how to not come unprepared to her environs. She had not intervened directly, but she was happy that the ling cod had escaped.

Although the cousins were a welcome change to their basic routine, Ray and his brother spent far more hours on the beach together. They gathered pollywogs from the swamp and raised them to watch them turn into frogs. Keeping them in buckets, they watched as the legs emerged and the pollywogs actually began to look more and more like frogs. When the frogs grew all their legs and lost their tails, they would walk down to the marsh and return the frogs to the environment of the pond.

They learned to create their own games, such as dashing along the beach, running only on the logs for as far as they could. The brother always won, since he was a head taller and his legs were much longer. He could jump the few gaps between the logs, while the boy had to look around for a longer route, where the logs were closer together.

They learned how to skip flat stones into the bay. The beach was loaded with rock shingle which had the perfect shape for a skipping stone. The boy's personal best was thirteen skips, but his brother, as usual outdid him and sent one rock skipping 21 times. Whenever the tide and weather conditions permitted, they waded into the eelgrass to look for crabs.

Catching crabs by hand is a special skill. He and his brother became very adept at capturing these creatures. A typical crab hunting expedition would be mounted with their own special kind of equipment. Each of them had polarized sunglasses to reach through the glare from the surface and look down into the sand and sea grass beds. They would tie five-gallon buckets to their waists with a little sea water to weigh them down and allowed them to trail along behind them. They each carried a stick. These expeditions typically took place in the late spring and early summer, when the crabs were aggressively mating and much more territorial. They would tap them with the stick and the crabs would rear back and threaten them with their claws. They teased them with the sticks until the crab grabbed a hold of the ends. Then they would hoist them out of the water and shake them into the bucket. If the crab was in shallow water, they would reach down and grasp their shell behind their claws and hoist them into the bucket.

Now, this may seem simple, but just like any hunt, you had to know the territory. Too much eel- grass, and you would never see the crabs unless you stepped on them, which is its own special thrill. Especially after Ray's father showed him how a crab could break a 1/2- inch stick with its claws, he was reticent about reaching down into the eelgrass blindly. Reaching down into the sediment which would be stirred up by their sticks and the scurrying crab, could be especially trying moment for anyone, since their claws could easily break a toe or injure their fingers if they reached down to find out what you had kicked. Many crabs would take off running for deeper water, when they were disturbed, and usually Ray never tried to stop them. He and his brother learned to scout the areas where the eel grass was thinner or between eelgrass beds, where the crabs would be heading for deeper water. Being able to see the larger crabs allowed you to go to full capture mode and get them into a bucket.

Because of the tendency for crabs to hide versus run, it was important to hunt them as the tide was going out. They seemed to sense the decreasing pressure of the water column and at a certain point realized that concealment was not going to protect them, but would instead leave them at the mercy of birds and flounders which hunted them also. They were not only much easier to spot when they were on the move, they were generally more aggressive. For their hunts they rarely used anything more than a broom handle. When they grabbed hold of the handle, they could then lift them into a bucket. Once in the bucket, it was important to determine if they were male or female. You sex a crab by looking at the underside of the crab. A rounded plate with only a slight peak is a female, while males come to a very distinctive point. The females were returned to the water. They could see the occasional crabber working from a boat in deeper water using a crab pot. This never seemed as sporting as their method, since it was kind of like netting large quantities of fish versus catching individual fish on a pole.

Because most of hunt was based upon visual cues, it was important to pick calm days, where waves had not stirred the sediment and reduced visibility. Using polarized sunglasses to work with the sun at their backs helped to penetrate the surface glare. It was a rare hunt where they did not return with at least a few Dungeness crabs and many red rock crabs. Their parents and friends were always very appreciative. They would see them later feasting on cracked crab and melted butter.

But gradually his brother turned elsewhere for his entertainment. He was a talented and athletic "three sports star" in both Junior and Senior High. This took up much of his time, since the activity bus drove nearly forty miles after his practices, before it came close enough to their area to drop him off. Some of his balance and athleticism could probably be traced by running along logs when he was young. Ray remembered specifically that he would jog along the beach with weights around his ankles, building both his strength and endurance.

Ray, on the other hand, turned inward. He could spend hours with Sophia, just listening to her inner voice and talking about the ocean, beach or marine animals. She was never quiet and always had something interesting to say. Her waves gently shushed him when he was disturbed or lonely. Her discussions challenged him to look into her hidden recesses and secrets to learn how she worked every day to provide homes for her diverse population. He still hopped logs down the beach, but he could just as easily sit on a log and watch as the tide went out and the waves changed their rhythms to the differing depths which became exposed. Just as Eagle had taught him, he became obsessed with finding out why things were the way they were along his beach. Sophia and he would have long conversations, but it usually led to some aspect of the beach and what he should learn about the interrelationships of the living things there. She would never tell him the answer, but she would keep prodding to ensure that he was looking for his own understanding. In other words, Sophia never gave her secrets easily, but if she was observed intently, she would give him clues on where to look to develop true insights into her depths.

She also allowed Ray time to just imagine and play. His brother had taught him a great game earlier in life, where they would shove small planks or pieces of wood into the bay and then try and hit them with rocks. All of his family had been involved in World War II, and several of his uncles had actually been on ships which were sunk. It didn't take long to envision that planks were aircraft carriers and small limbs were cruisers or destroyers. Then the beach would offer the perfect size rocks to be throw skyward to fall like dive bombs, or round rocks which could be used as main gun batteries. He even used skipping stones to mimic torpedoes. The tide and waves could be counted upon to make hitting any piece of wood at a distance, very difficult but not impossible. He credited this training along with his brother for teaching him how to pitch in baseball. For the rest of his life, he could throw any ball and hit any target with ease.

So, from the time he was five onwards he had free run with his friend. As long as his homework and chores were done and he told his Mom where he was going, he could be gone for hours. These were different times, than the present. The entire family was isolated from everyone, so there was little chance he would somehow be abducted. He grew up expecting that he could go just about anywhere in safety. Sometimes he would just walk, looking for good stuff which had washed up, like kelp whips or sealed cans. Other times, Ray would just sit on a log and watch as the beach changed before his eyes. He had favorite spots, where he could lay with his head cradled by one log, with his feet up on the next. He also learned not to lay in sandy areas, since they were usually infested with sand-fleas. Although, they did not bite, it felt all creepy crawly to have them swarm onto his body.

Just like the perch which he threw back, he never brought home animal life for his personal consumption. It just didn't seem right to take something from Sophia for his personal use. He could dig for clams, get crab or geoducks, as long as it was for the thrill of the catch and for someone else to eat, but he never partook of the food sources. He loved shrimp and lobster, and they were not under the protection of Sophia. Even when he went hunting for crabs or clams, he always made sure he thanked her for her largess, before going back to his house. Now, he could bring his friends or family and Sophia would tolerate their gathering clams, crabs or geoducks, but he always felt that she was just being neighborly. It was okay, but she didn't like people who just took advantage of her resources. It was always her goal to try and teach more fundamentals about her ways, in addition to just digging up clams. He learned how important it was to refill the holes which were dug in the beach and to limit the handling of a sea cucumber to avoid its regurgitation.

Sophia was always enticing him to learn new and deeper secrets. As an example, they found hundreds of unusual rubber-feeling casings in the sandy areas of the beach. He struggled for years wondering what these could be. They had both a sandy texture and a rubber feeling to the shape. It was possible to bend them and tear them. After several years, he finally discovered that they were the egg cases from moon snails which lived in the tidal zone. Each casing contains thousands of moon snail eggs. Moon snails are not sweet pearlescent creatures which might rally to the aid of a Disney heroine. Moon snails are vicious nocturnal predators. If you are a bivalve, you do not want to encounter a moon snail in a dark alley or mud flat.

If you are a bivalve and you do encounter a moon snail in a dark mud flat, expect to have a hole bored through your shell faster than a clam can say whatever it is clams say when they are about to die. Moon snails are equipped with a power-drilling rasp and lethal corrosive acid secretions.

After the hole is drilled there is a brief period as the clam is being sucked through a hole and eaten alive, without even the dignity of a lemon wedge. As a clam goes, moon snails and starfish are their main predators. He thought as deaths go; he preferred the moon snails over the Starfish. The starfish senses chemicals which are released into the water by its prey. Just as anyone can follow the smell of a hot apple pie to the kitchen, the starfish can follow the "smell" of a clam, mussel, or oyster. By the time the starfish finds it, the clam has probably closed its shell tightly. A closed clam is almost impossible to open, but a starfish takes its time. It latches onto the clam shell and uses its hundreds of tiny, tube-shaped feet which work like suction cups. And then it pulls. A starfish can pull for days if necessary. After a while, the clam gets tired. It opens its shell a tiny bit.

Then the starfish does something else which seems almost impossible. Because starfish have no teeth, they cannot bite the clam. Instead, they are much more insidious. It pushes one of its two stomachs out through its mouth and into the clam's shell. Inside the shell, this stomach swallows the clam's soft body. They must make their food soupy before they can eat it. The stomach makes juices which dissolve the clam. For final digestion, the starfish sucks the clam soup into its second stomach, which always stays inside its body. Then the starfish crawls away, leaving an empty shell behind. A large starfish can consume 50 clams in a week.

Now, Sophia told him something which he found hard to believe. She said "Starfish attacked mainly buried clams. Those species that can move like razor clams or scallops, could escape from starfish." Especially scallops because they actually had eyes and would see the Starfish approach and then escape by clapping their shells together.

First, he looked up scallops and found to his surprise that they indeed did have eyes along the edge of the shells. After reading about scallops, he decided to test whether this was an escape mechanism for just scallops or for other bivalves. He and the beach found a small tide pool about 1 foot by two feet. They put a starfish in the pool. Finding a cockle clam, which has a large three-inch foot, he placed it near the starfish. In less than two minutes, the cockle was extending its' huge foot and jumping away from the starfish. It finally left the tide pool. Despite that one ability to escape, Sophia illustrated how successful these hunters were. She was littered with thousands of clam shells with holes and without holes, testifying to the voracious nature of these predators. She did not seem to care, which group predominated. She just provided the environment and let them interact with each other. It was much later in college, where Ray realized how the system maintained its balance within the predation environment which had been established. And that a powerful image was being created in his mind where there were no ultimate winners and losers in life, but just interactions which could lead to good things or bad. She was providing him with her wisdom to accept situations which were not within his control and were not ever meant to be within the control of anyone.

Sophia realized that he was an unusual child, in that he was much more inquisitive than anyone else she had met. She kept feeding him conundrums and questions to keep him occupied. Ray didn't realize until much later how she was leading him towards a college degree and a career. She stoked the fires of his lifelong need to know how systems worked and the basis for how things interact. It was the beginning of his personal search for universal truth and enlightenment.

Unusual Animals

Part of the fascination of Sophia was her endless surprises. Ray's first exposure to death was found on the beach, where a sea lion carcass had washed up on shore. He was only six, but the carcass was huge and bloated and covered with thousands of sand fleas and flies. Except for the flippers and the head, it would have been difficult to identify what it really had been. Now it was food for bugs, crabs, and bacteria. It was located almost next to the head of the dock. The Navy presence was still there at the time and they attached ropes to the flippers and winched it off the beach and then towed it into deeper water and sank it with gunshots to the now inflated body. It sank into the depths and the smell gradually dissipated in the area.

The next item found washed up on shore was a four-foot skate. A skate is a relative of the shark, but has been flattened out to allow it hide on the bottom and search for its favorite foods such as cockles, shrimp or crabs. They took pictures of it and searched the tail to see if it was a sting ray (it wasn't), and then dragged it back to the waves to allow Sophia and her friends to take care of it.

Since the Sound is a major port entrance, they also found many items washed off of ships which were deposited on shore. Ray discovered one bottle with a note in it from a Swedish sailor, a 12 lb. tin of Canadian coffee, and many other items which he always lugged back to his house to see if his parents wanted them. Most were thrown off the bluff.

One day as Ray walked along in a deep discussion with Sophia, he looked up and less than ten feet away was a sea otter staring back at him. Ray was so surprised, his jaw dropped. The otter looked like this was an everyday occurrence. For 10 seconds or so, they just looked each other up and down. The otter quickly became bored and just walked out into the waves. He surfaced about twenty feet from shore and continued to examine Ray. Every so often, he would look under the waves and then resurface on his back like he was in an easy chair and just watch some more. One time, he came up with a huge red rock crab. He had one claw in his mouth and had pinned the other claw to his chest with one hand. He proceeded to devour the claw, then deftly switched the other claw into his mouth. He nibbled away at the legs, until finally there was nothing left but the body. He peeled that open and devoured the eggs and soft tissue inside. He had done all of this so easily, like he was munching on potato chips watching TV. He then took off to the south, where the kelp beds were and Ray never saw him again. But he could always recall the magic of that moment, where he saw the ease of life for some denizens of the beach.

Although many things routinely washed up on shore, certainly most memorable was the 18-foot shark which ended up right below his house on the beach. Sand sharks or dogfish are endemic to the sound, but nobody thought that large sharks lived in the cold waters of the Sound. When his parents and neighbors would go salmon fishing, they inevitably caught a few of these 4–5-foot dogfish. But the shark which washed up on the beach was totally different.

At this time no one had an idea that any sharks of this size lived in Puget Sound. If fact, it looked very unusual, in that it no dorsal fin and had only six gills. Ray being the inquisitive one, cut out several teeth and one of the eyes. The eye in particular looked enormous, bigger than his fist and it would reflect light from inside the eye. His parents contacted the high school biology teacher, who wasn't interested. They finally did some research and found references to a six-gill shark. Much later it was discovered that they are one of the main shark species in Puget Sound, but normally lived so deep that they were rarely ever seen. His Mom located a source of formalin to encase the eye and the teeth. As usual, Ray took them to school to prepare for show and tell. His mom was learning to not allow him to take rotting stuff to school for show and tell, thus storing them in the formalin. He really wanted to cut open the shark and look at the contents of the stomach, but his parents vetoed the idea and the tough skin would probably have defeated his efforts anyway. Sharkskin is both incredibly tough but is also abrasive. It is actually many small teeth facing backwards along the length of the shark. He had to be very careful not to brush his bare hand along its surface, as it could easily abrade the skin off his hands and fingers.

As the great body began to decay, the stench from in front of house became more and more unbearable. Finally, his Dad borrowed a neighbor's boat, attached a meat hook to 1/2 inch line and towed it off the beach. Ray went with him and they cruised around, hoping that one of the kicker boat fishermen which routinely fished for salmon in front of their house would ask "How's the fishing?" No one ever did and after an hour they finally cut the rope and the great fish sank out of sight into the deep waters of the Sound.

Octopus had sat in his rocky home in the depths and thought and thought about how to teach Ray about sentiency of many of the animals of the beach. After 12 years, he thought he had a way of explaining it the most personal terms possible. Octopus' girlfriend was pregnant. And female octopuses die almost immediately after birth. He spoke to her and asked her to help. If she would allow herself to be captured and studied at the Marine Science Center, where Ray spent many of his high school days, she could show him how intelligent she was. After some thought, she agreed.

When she was brought into the lab and placed in a special tank she weighed well over 80 pounds. Like the other students Ray spent hours studying her behavior. He could even see her watching him with her deep-set eyes. One late afternoon, she reached out a tentacle and touched Ray gently on the hand. She spoke directly to him by touch. She explained that tonight was the full moon and she would be giving birth, and then she would die. She did not wish to poison the water with her death, so she asked Ray to leave the cover open just a crack. That night she reached out with a tentacle and gently pulled open the locking hasp on the lid, crawled through facility, opened another door and then escaped to the bay, leaving thousands of eggs attached to the tank. Ray was fascinated and gained a new found respect for all life and its intelligence.

The Rescues

The Sound where the beach is located could be quite dangerous. It can start out as a gloriously sunny day and two hours later, the wind is blowing 45 knots and 6–8-foot waves called white caps arrive. Couple this with frigidly cold water and a potential for rain, and you have the origin of a difficult environment for the unprepared. The old dock and breakwater were perfectly placed as a haven of safety during many of the storms. Most storms in the Sound originate in the south and come sweeping up along the length of the Sound gaining strength as it flows up the channels. With its natural curvature and the dock, it provided some protection from these southerlies.

When his parents first built the house above the beach, they had not set the glass in the picture windows. During the morning the sun was out and it was nice and warm during that particular spring day, but around 4 PM, the winds started to pick up, and they could see the white caps beginning to form in the bay. Most of the fisherman, in their small boats, used this early indicator to head for home. Some of the small boats did not leave immediately and one in particular stayed way too long.

The storm continued to pick up energy and waves begin to crest at around 6 feet. It was also extremely choppy, with waves not coming in swells, but rapidly from several directions at once. Now they finally saw some action on the last boat. It was obvious that their engine was undersized for the effort needed. They struggled to try and get behind the wing walls of the dock. They made at least nine attempts, and each one ended with them being swept on past the dock. Finally, they got in just the right position and gunned the engine to enter into the inner area of the dock. As everyone watched through their binoculars they seemed to heave a sigh of relief.

They tied up to one of the pilings, and then each of the three men on board dropped their pants and peed over the side of the boat, and gave what looked like a long sigh of relief. Ray could hear Sophia explode in a paroxysm of laughter. In the morning the winds had calmed and they were gone. But those particular fishermen were famous on the shoreline for evermore.

The very next year, the family was once again sitting at the house site, with one of the two permanent families along this stretch of Beach, enjoying a barbecue. They noticed that once again it was starting to get a little windy out on the water. During the day, it had been sunny and probably 50 small recreational fishing boats had been in front of the house trolling back and forth for salmon. As the winds picked up most of these boats took off for their harbors. All except one, who just seemed to be just sitting out in the bay.

Ray's father picked up his binoculars, and could see the occupants sitting in the boat looking dejected with the cover off their outboard engine. He realized that they were in trouble. So, the neighbor and Ray's brother took off to get the neighbor's boat launched. They had a boathouse down on the beach and could roll the boat directly into the surf. While they struggled to launch the boat, Ray's Mom called the Coast Guard and told them that there was a boat in trouble and the location. Within ten minutes a Coast Guard plane arrived, with the distinctive white body and red stripe, circling above the boat. They could see the kicker boat leaving the beach and heading for the stricken boat. It was not more than 150 yards away. The plane flew back to Seattle and then reappeared just above the water. It was flying low and using its prop wash to flatten the waves, and just leaving Seattle, about ten miles away was a Coast Guard cutter. The plane roared over the small kicker boat, then pulled up and over Ray's house and then back down on the deck in front of the small kicker boat. It was flattening the waves for them also. It made a long axis figure eight and made three total passes over the each of the would-be rescuers. Each time the waves would be flattened by the prop wash. The kicker boat arrived only minutes before the cutter. Pretty good considered they had to go 150 yards and the cutter had sped across the ten-mile crossing in about the same time.

As his brother stood in the bow, he saw that the people in the little boat had engine parts scattered from one end of the boat to the other. He had the nerve to ask them, "How's fishing?" They didn't think it very funny. They had been trying to signal all of the little boats in the area, by waving seat cushions and yelling. Each of the other boats waved back and then took off for home, not realizing their predicament. When the cutter arrived, they took the people on board and attached a tow line to bring the little boat home. The last they saw of the plane was when they waggled their wings and headed back to their base.

Periodically, people would come out to spend the summer along the beach. They saw the enormous quantities of clams available and would go crazy eating them with butter and garlic. They didn't follow some of the checks which locals automatically keep in mind. It was common practice to check the hotline and papers to check on the periodic blooms of dinoflagellates or the "red tide". Clams would gorge themselves on this bloom, and as part of consumption would break apart the plankton. The shells of these type of plankton, would become lodged in the clam's flesh, especially butter clams. People would eat the clams, but would not recognize the telltale signs, so would continue to consume the clams. Too much eventually causes paralysis of the diaphragm and if not treated immediately leads to death, as the person stops breathing. At least once every three to four years, one of the summer people would succumb to this and cause quite a stir. Locals became quite adept at contacting ambulance support, while keeping the person breathing as normally as possible.

Although the next tale is not strictly a rescue, it was still an unusual boating incident. It was a dark and stormy night, and as Ray looked out the windows, there appeared a beautiful sailboat sailing perpendicular to the teeth of a storm. The wind was from the south, and the boat was sailing close to the wind. It just barely cleared the old dock, but he could see that it was heading directly for the beach. As everyone hustled outside, they heard the grinding noise of a boat hitting the beach rocks. They could just see the mast as it rose up onto the shoreline and the sails went limp. Running down to the beach, to help as best they could, they found the boat was empty.

The next day it was discovered, that a woman had sailed the boat all the way from Edmonds, about 20 miles against the wind and put that sailboat on the beach like she knew exactly what she was doing. She claimed that her husband had been knocked overboard and she did not know what to do, so she sailed it onto the rocks. He had left his wallet, Rolex watch, and personal flotation device on board, which seemed to indicate, that there might be more to the story. Also, the woman, did not seem overly upset over the loss of her husband and simply asked to use the phone to report the accident. The boat was salvaged the next day and no one ever heard of her again nor any repercussions for the incident. Now, it is difficult to put a sailboat on the shore into the teeth of a storm, but it was her calm and placid behavior which seemed to indicate a deeper background story than they heard.

The dock was also a sight of some unusual situations. One day an old minesweeper showed up tied to the south wing-wall. It was rumored that the owner planned on refitting her as a pleasure boat. Unfortunately, where he tied it up, there were some sunken pilings which at low tide eventually punctured the hull and the minesweeper settled below the surface. Since it was just below the surface and could take out the bottom of sailboats or any deeper hulled vessel, the Coast Guard finally placed a buoy above the wreck. The buoy had a flashing light and a bell with four clappers which rang constantly. Whenever the buoy rocked, the bell would sound. It drove all the residents of the beach crazy, to the point of distraction when you were trying to sleep with the windows open. Ray finally took some old nylons from his Mother and tied up the clappers to stop the ringing. The sunken minesweeper became an infamous dive sight on the beach.

One day, Ray heard the bell begin ringing again. Thinking that he would have to row out and reattach the nylons, he checked out the buoy through binoculars. There were two divers lying on the buoy. One was waving his mask and snorkel trying to get someone's attention. He ran down to the beach and pushed the family dinghy over the logs and rowed out to see what was going on. The waves were getting serious and it was difficult to row his plastic dinghy on a calm day, but he finally approached the buoy. One of the divers kept saying "Thank God". The other was almost passed out and could hardly move. Ray threw a line to the one diver and they tied up to the buoy.

Together they managed to get his friend into the boat and then he brought all of their equipment; air tanks, weight belts buoyancy compensators, etc., into that little dinghy. His friend was almost incoherent, but they explained that they were from southern California. They had driven all night to get to the beach to see the minesweeper shipwrecked there. The cold water had come as a complete shock to them, and his friend had been overcome by the biting cold of the water. Sophia did not tolerate stupidity for any length of time. Managing to row them back to the beach, Sophia seemed to be whispering to him; "See what I do to the unprepared". He helped the exhausted diver up to the logs and got him some food from their backpacks. After he stowed the dinghy, they were standing and picking up their stuff to return to their car. The one diver seemed to be recovering. After they left, Ray found some of the equipment which they had left behind, such as a snorkel and depth indicator. No one ever heard from them again, no "Thank you" or reward. They probably just returned to

California with a story which they could tell concerning friends how cold it was in the Northwest waters.

The final rescue was actually so dangerous, because of the singular nature of the situation. Ray had fallen in love with the image of diving. It gave him new insights into Sophia, in that he could see and explore below the surface, while the tide was in. He had taken classes from top Navy divers, and received his certification for scuba. He had purchased the top-of-the-line wet suit which allowed for significant time for exploration without hypothermia setting in. But since he was a teenager, he also had the hubris of thinking himself to be immortal and not subject to common sense rules. He decided one day to anchor the dinghy to use it to store any crabs which he caught. He floated through the eelgrass, and had caught several large rock crabs, when he spotted a huge Dungeness crab heading for deeper water.

He was not wearing his weight belt, so with his own natural buoyancy coupled with the float associated with the wet suit, he was pinned to very close to the surface. He decided to return to the boat, grab the anchor and use it to take him down low enough to grab that Dungeness crab.

All was working out perfectly, until he dropped the anchor near the crab, and the slack in the line wrapped itself around his right leg. Now he was pinned between his and the boat's buoyancy, and the weight of the anchor. He also, realized which despite all of his training, he had left his knife in the boat. (His instructors had told him that he should shower with his knife). The anchor had imbedded itself in an eelgrass bed and could not be jerked free. He was trapped below the surface unable to surface or go down to the anchor. He actually thought of his parents searching for him and finding himself suspended and dead in the anchor line.

> *At just that moment, Sophia came to his rescue.*
> *She said "Calm down, quit struggling, and exhale the remaining air from your lungs". Although this seemed to be the opposite of what he should do, she told him, "You can hold your breath for over three minutes, you'll make it.*

He did exactly what she said to do, and by expelling the air, he reduced his buoyancy enough where he could pull himself upside down and managed to unwrap the double loop from his legs. He swam to the surface and said a silent prayer for the friendship which had saved his life.

The Cousins Again

Although Ray's fathers' family occasionally visited them it was a rare occurrence. Usually about every five years they would either visit his dad's brother in Denver, or the brothers (he had two) would come to visit us at the beach. Their kids were much older than Ray and were definitely not interested in the beach. In comparison, his Mom's family seemed to get together all of the time. She had a sister who was only one year younger than she, and their babies were born at near the same time. They grew up in Olympia, and either they would go to their house or they would come to the beach and stay with Ray and his family. In addition to this sister, Ray's mom had two older siblings and a younger brother. The older siblings rarely visited us, but sometimes her younger brother would come to our house. He had four kids, younger than Ray. They were also city kids.

The cousins from Olympia were country folk and enjoyed the beach. The country cousins loved to fish, dig clams and geoducks and were not afraid to get their hands dirty. Ray and his brother both loved it when they came to visit. All of them would start by fishing from the dock and if the tide was low enough, proceed to dig clams and get crabs and have a great big dinner of seafood. Ray, as was his way, always remembered to thank Sophia for her largesse.

Ray's moms' younger brother would never ride across the ferries. His wife was deathly afraid of any boat or ship travel. So, when they came to visit, they had had to drive around from North Seattle, all the way through Tacoma and then up to Ray's house. This was about a four-hour trip at the best of times. Worse if the weather or traffic was not good. By the time those city kids arrived at our house they had a ton of pent-up energy and attitudes which were not pleasant to be around. As a group, did not particularly care for Sophia or for the activities which could be done on the beach. Sophia actually resented them and their attitudes and did her best to make their visits not very enjoyable.

One day they came over and it was bright and sunny summer day. Everyone wanted to go fishing from the dock. Ray pointed out to his dad, that he only had three hand lines for essentially five people. Ray offered to not fish, but that still left them a fishing line with a line short. His father decided to let the oldest cousin, who was around ten at the time use his expensive salmon pole and reel. They all trudged down to the beach, where they proceeded to catch the perch from the dock. Ray quickly sensed that the cousin, with the salmon pole, was getting bored with fishing. He told everyone that the next fish he caught, he was going to show everybody a big surprise.

About five minutes later he hooked a big perch and took the salmon pole and threw it into the bay. He almost did not survive to reach eleven years old, because Ray's father was ready to throw him after it. Instead, everyone just quit fishing and went back to the house. Sophia hated waste in any form, and Ray always thought that she took that fishing pole and hid it. Every low tide from that point on, they would look for that fishing pole, but never found it.

When everyone went back to the house, two of the cousins were sharing a small telescope to look at the ships going by in the channel. They were taking turns, when the one who had the telescope had to go to the bathroom. When he got back, he looked through the telescope and then leaned back and decked his brother. He said, "When I left, I had a boat in there and you let it go". These were the same cousins who asked if they turned the waves off at night.

This was actually a very common theme which seemed to occur when people had not grown up around the ocean as Ray had. The family had friends from Montana which were coming to visit. When they finally arrived in Seattle to catch the ferry, one of their three kids asked when they could hear the sound. His parents said "What sound?" He said "You know, the Puget Sound!" It took many discussions with them before they believed that their parents were not pulling their legs. Given all of these occurrences it is fairly reasonable to understand how those newbies were confused by Sophia and her ways.

One day as Ray was walking long her shores, Sophia said to him: "I enjoy your family and friends, but my favorite time is just walking with you and having you to myself." Ray replied, "I know what you mean, they exhaust me, but you exhilarate me in ways which I never thought possible."

Their souls reached out and touched and they spent the day just walking along her domain and seeing life as it went about its daily business of living.

Gathering her Resources

Ray became adept at finding Sophia's hidden sources of life which were enjoyed by humans as an edible item on any menu. As mentioned before, he and his brother would wade out at low tides to find crabs. Crabs are wily critters and cunning in their use of natural concealment and the other forms of life to hide behind. The north point was one generally good location as well as the tidal pool to the south of the dock. By working as a pair of hunters, they could scour most of the beach. Ray would work the inshore areas, while his brother worked the deeper portions.

In comparison, clam digging is almost too easy. As long as the tide was low enough, they could always find clams. They existed in bands along the beach's shoreline. During any low tide, they could normally access the first two bands of clams. The third band was far more problematic and required not only an extremely low tide, but some specialized equipment as well. The first band was just below the shingled layer and where rocks, sand and anemones mixed along the shore. Although the digging could be hard, they used to start the hole with a shovel and then switch to a long tined rake. To find the clams, you simply raked the edges of the hole. Rocks and small steamer clams would fall from the side of the hole into the water in the bottom of the hole. You reached into the water and rinsed off the clams and ensured that they were alive and not shells full of mud. Then they just placed them in a bucket. It is also extremely important to fill in the holes which you dig to ensure that you do not open the clam beds to additional predation by removing cover over the clams.

The types of clams found in this shore band are manila or littleneck clams. In both species the crosshatching of the rings on the shells is very evident. Manila Clams were accidentally introduced to Washington State in oyster seed shipments from Japan. The animal quickly acclimated to our waters and is now found from British Columbia to northern California. They are similar in size and appearance to littlenecks; however, they are oblong in shape, being longer than the rounded littlenecks. The internal surface of the shells near the siphon end is normally stained a deep purple color or yellow.

The shells completely close. Their siphons are short so they are buried to only about 4" fairly high in the intertidal zone. They inhabit a variety of substrates, from gravel to mud to sand, above the half-tide level, which is higher than the zone where butter and littleneck clams are found. The black siphon tips on Manilas are split. The inside edge of their shell is smooth to the touch.

In Puget Sound, they are especially abundant in small outlets and lagoons. Growth is quite rapid with the clams reaching marketable size in two years or less. This species has become a welcome addition to Washington's list of clams and is taken commercially by hand diggers and by sport diggers with shovels, forks and rakes. It is a shallow burrower with many found within the first two inches of substrate, and for this reason is easily harvested by hand-digging. Manilas account for 50 per cent of the annual commercial landings of hard-shell clams in Washington.

Littlenecks are similar in appearance to the manila clam and differ only in the shape of the shell itself. The manila is oblong, while the littleneck is more rounded in appearance. The variable, but external surface is marked with concentric rings and radiating ridges which produce a cross-hatched appearance. The color is normally cream or grey, and sometimes mottled with brown markings. They have an external hinge ligament and the black siphon tips of native littlenecks are fused together. The inside edge of their shell has a fine, toothed- edge, easily seen and felt. They are found in the top 4-6 inches of substrate of gravel-mud in protected bays. Sport diggers normally use rakes, shovels or forks to obtain them. On very rare occasions they can form pearls. They are delicious when steamed open and dipped in hot butter.

The next band of shoreline includes butter clams and horse clams. They are found primarily in the sandy areas of the beach. Butter clams are about three times larger than the littleneck/manila steamer clams. Their shells show only concentric rings with no crosshatching like the steamer clams.

The horse clams are usually five to ten times larger still. So, when Ray was done digging for steamers, he would follow the tide out to the sandier areas of the beach looking for the tell-tale small holes where the clam's bivalve structure would penetrate the surface and leave a hole where water had been siphoned or expelled until the zone was exposed by the low tide. They used a similar technique to find the clams, but it was necessary to dig down about 8-12 inches to properly expose the living zone of the clams. They would then rake the sides of the hole, looking for the pale beige of the shells.

Tides in Puget Sound could be 15-17 feet. To access the third band of clams, usually required a good low tide. During the summer these would occur about every other week for 2 months. During these low tides, Ray's family would dig for geoducks. Many people believed at the time that geoducks dig down into the soft sand when digging them up, like razor clams. But in reality, the shell is located 2 1/2 to 3 feet below the sand surface. When they sense danger, they retract the necks and expand their shell bodies to resist removal.

The geoduck is one of the largest clams in the world, weighing in at an average of one to three pounds at maturity, but some weighing over 15 pounds and as much as 6.5 feet in length could be found. Geoducks have a life expectancy of over 100 years. Experts told Ray that the geoduck's lengthy age is the result of low wear and tear. A geoduck sucks water containing Phyto- and zoo-plankton down through its long siphon, filters this for food and ejects its refuse out through a separate hole in the siphon. And adult geoducks have few predators, which may also contribute to their longevity.

Although they can be dug using only shovels, this can be extremely difficult as the edges of the hole continually wash into the center of the pit being dug. Retracting their neck places the body of the clam very deep within the hole. To retrieve these clams' people cannot just grasp the neck and pull since this will typically just break a portion of the neck off in their hands and kill the geoduck. It is necessary to work your hands deep into the holes and grasp the upper portion of the shell and gradually wiggle it loose from the sediment.

Ray's Dad was used to digging razor clams along the Washington Ocean coast and had seen clam guns which could be inserted over the razor clam and then remove sand and clam from their natural environment. He designed a heavy duty can about 3 1/2 feet long with an internal diameter of at least two feet. He also drilled two holes at the top, where a pipe could be inserted.

When the neck of the geoduck was located, they would sink the can around the neck with the clam centered in the middle. By digging out the sand from the interior of the can the top of the shell can be exposed. Ray's Mom would go down inside the can, grab the shell of the geoduck and wiggle it loose. It took about 15 minutes per clam to dig. But the clam was considered to be such a delicacy, that it was worth the effort.

In order to get the maximum number of three geoducks, they each had their individual assignments. Ray's Dad would stand on the pipes to push the clam tube into the sand and dig out the area between the sides of the can and the geoduck. His Mom's job was to enter the can and wiggle lose the geoduck from the sand encasing the shell. His Dad would then hold onto one leg to keep her from falling in over her head. There were usually neighbors or relatives which could also help with the digging. Ray's job was to roam the sand bar looking for the telltale signs of the geoduck neck. He would walk the sand bar and mark the locations with a stick or flag, to allow the diggers to avoid any extra effort.

Much later in his life, he learned that geoduck beds were huge in Puget Sound. That several thousand pounds of geoducks could be harvested by divers utilizing hoses blowing water away from the neck. During Ray's college career, he actually worked in a geoduck factory where they would cut the hard muscles away from the main body of the clam and then prepare them for use by restaurants. The best and most tender young geoducks were frozen solid and shipped to Japan for sashimi or sushi. Now the very first person which ate a geoduck had to be brave indeed. They just do not look that appetizing when seen in the wild.

As an aside, both of Ray's daughters, who went to college, attended the Evergreen State College. Their mascot is the Fighting Geoduck. Below is their fight song.

Go, Geoducks go, Through the mud and the sand,
let's go.
Siphon high, squirt it out, swivel all about,
let it all hang out. Go, Geoducks go,
Stretch your necks when the tide is low
Siphon high, squirt it out, swivel all about, let it
all hang out.

The preparation of each species of clams required some specific techniques. The littleneck and manila clams could be steamed open immediately and dipped in butter for consumption. Butter clams needed some time to spit out sand from the stomachs and siphons. They would soak them in seawater overnight with a dusting of corn meal. The clams would filter out the corn meal from the water and expel the sand from their systems.

Ray heard many of the old-timers along the beach complain about the toughness of the geoduck meat. One day he carried one around all day by the neck, and watched it stretch back to its original length. When his Dad cooked it that evening, he commented on how tender it was. From that point on, his Dad made it a point to stretch the necks out, finding that the trunk of a Buick worked like a champ. Since the Japanese and Chinese markets opened, geoducks have become a huge industry; providing a revenue stream in the 100s of millions of dollars. Harvests are being monitored to ensure that the huge beds of geoducks remain sustainable. Plus, many geoducks are over 100 years old. They are still considered to be the king of all clams, and when properly prepared are the most tender of all clams. You can see that some diggers used the trunk of an old car on occasion for the stretching to take place. The neck meat changed dramatically from being very tough to becoming extremely tender. As soon as the neck relaxed, they would have a pot of boiling water on hand. Using a knife, they severed the two muscles holding the shell to the body, cut off the racquet ball sized stomach and then dipped the entire geoduck in the pot of boiling water. Pulling it back out within 15-20 seconds, the exterior skin could then be removed like pulling off a nylon stocking. The meat was then a dazzling white or pale yellow. Ray's Dad preferred to make them into chowder or fritters (pancakes). The meat around the shell could be tenderized with a mallet and then fried in a skillet. When the feast was over, once again Ray did not participate, he would return the shells to the beach.

Unusual Denizens of the Beach

Everyone could always find jellyfish, starfish, clams, crabs and perch along the beach, but often Ray would run across something new and unusual. Given the hours he spent with Sophia, this is probably understandable. She was always throwing him a new curve to keep his interest pique. Some of these, were so unusual, he would spend days looking for their name and what they were. These were like the gumboot chitons, limpets, nudibranchs, sea cucumbers, sea pens, ratfish, and one time which he still recalls with trepidation; a Cabazon. However, the first animal he ever saw that truly perplexed him was a sea cucumber. They had a superficial resemblance to a cucumber in size, but that is where the similarity stopped. They had rows of tiny tube feet, a mouth, and gills. He first picked one up and showed a friend the tube feet underneath. They were moving like a wave and shared some characteristics of the starfish. As he was moving it around, it suddenly began to quiver and then the insides became the outsides as it expelled a disgusting muddle of digested products along with the stomach and intestines. He thought that somehow, he had killed it. After significant research, Ray found out that they also had a nasty habit of expelling their insides if they were handled too much. He learned later that this was a real but unusual defense mechanism, in which any predator would choose to eat this regurgitated matter, while the sea cucumber raced to safety on her tiny tube feet. They moved almost as fast as a snail. They would then re-grow a set of stomach and intestines to return to their lives. They can be cut open and there are six long muscles growing along their length which can be eaten. That simply did not seem appetizing to anyone in his family, so they typically left them alone, except to show new people.

One of the strangest fish, Ray saw was hooked once by one of his cousins from the dock. This was the ratfish. It had both an unusual shape, but one set of fins were long and bony and were used like feet along the bottom. This was the ratfish. After quickly looking at it external taxonomy, it was returned to the depths from whence it came. Flounders could be found all along the beach. They look like miniature halibut and taste quite delicious. They also have a defense mechanism where they can change their background coloration to closely match the surface upon which the rest. Although, when they are first hatched, they look like normal fish, their eyes gradually move until both of them eyes are located on the top of the fish.

The unusual capability to change their colors to match their backgrounds can be quite striking. Normally, they are sandy colored when floating along a sandy stretch of beach or quickly change to a mottled back when floating above a rocky shore. While Ray was wading along the shoreline talking to the beach, a flounder actually swam up to him. Usually, they are skittish and hightail it to the deeper part of the bay as soon as they sense any potential predator. This one was completely unafraid. In fact, he could gently stroke its back and its thin sides and it would swim alongside him whenever he waded into the eelgrass. It was not spooked by Ray at all, but seemed to enjoy the attention of being scratched and returned to swim alongside of Ray for several weeks. Ray felt that Sophia had told the flounder that he was not dangerous and was fun to play with, so the flounder enjoyed the attention and would seek out Ray, whenever he was wading. One day, the beach had a number of both fishermen and beachcombers. Ray's friend the flounder did not return to his side that day. He always had a feeling that it had been picked up and carried away by these people. He has never had or even heard of a similar situation with a human being and a flounder.

One of the oddest denizens was the gumboot chiton. The thing was the size of a football and weighed twice as much. When Ray found it, he picked it up, wondering "What in the hell is this?" Underneath it had a foot like a snail but was bigger than his hand. While Ray handled it started to curl up like a hedgehog. After his experience with the sea cucumber, he quickly returned it to the tide pool where they had found it. The gumboot chiton is usually found clinging to rocks, moving slowly in search of its diet of algae or seaweed scraped off of rocks with its rasp-like retractable radula. This rasp is covered with rows of very sharp teeth. Active at night, the gumboot generally feeds at this time and often remains in a hiding place during the day. The gumboot can live for over 40 years. It has few natural predators, the most common being other snail, although the snail's efforts to consume the chiton are generally limited to the outer mantle only. Other predators are the octopus, starfish and sea otters.

Sea pens could be seen in the great tidal pool south of the dock in front of the degaussing station. There you could find veritable forests of pens fanning the water for plankton. As octocorals, sea pens are colonial animals which look like miniature sea anemones. However, a sea pen's polyps are specialized to specific functions: a single polyp develops into a rigid, erect stalk and loses its tentacles, forming a bulbous "root" at its base. The other polyps branch out from this central stalk and feed structures with stinging cells. Using their root- like peduncles to anchor themselves in the sand, they fan the sea for plankton. Their primary predators are sea slugs and starfish, some of which feed exclusively on sea pens.

Limpets, also called China-man hats or opihi in Hawaiian do resemble the old Hollywood vision of a Chinese peasant hat. The limpet is a relative of a snail. A limpet has one big foot and a strong suction cup. Limpets eat only at night because then they are much safer moving around. Limpets eat algae off rocks using their radula or mouth-scraper. Limpets always go back to the same place after eating. Sometimes they use the same spot for their whole life. Limpets fit back into their place in the rock perfectly. Limpets can find their way back to their rock home. They leave a trail of mucus behind them, like pebbles in the story of Hansel and Gretel, which chemically "stores" a history of their travels. They use sensitive chemical receptors to find their way back by "reading" the trail. If Ray touched them, they would clamp down hard onto the rock and their shells actually fit into a home groove which an older limpet would have created by constant usage. He used a knife to slip under the edge and break the suction to remove it. They are considered to be a delicacy in Hawaii, so one day he collected some to serve at a Luau. He put the container in the refrigerator to wait for the party. When he opened the refrigerator the next day, he found that they had escaped the container and were scattered throughout the fridge.

Ray and his Mom took out the dinghy one day, to explore the wing wall of the dock. This is a structure to break up waves prior to reaching the actual dock itself. As they were floating along, they saw a bright yellow body undulating from a n-shape to a smile. It was swimming by alternating contracting the muscles on the bottom and then the top of the organism. It had gills at one end and antennae at the other. By this time, they were both quite experienced in unusual animals which could be found on the beach. They held it gently in their hands and could sense the muscled foot of the animal pulsing to move along their outstretched fingers. They returned it to the wing wall and looked it up in their marine taxonomy book and found that it met all of the parameters of a sea lemon or nudibranch, a type of snail. They marveled at both the concept of a snail with no shell and its bright yellow color. They found out later that it was advertising that it tasted bad and was left alone by most predators along the beach.

As Ray continued to explore as he grew older, he found that he desired to see more of the beach's natural inhabitants at other than low tide. Low tides are especially stressful events for most of these organisms and he wanted to observe their behavior in a more natural condition. As mentioned previously he took classes and became certified as a scuba diver. He also invested in a wet suit to try and keep the chill of the water from ruining his enjoyment of these observations. Although he was certified to use scuba tanks, he found this involved three times as much equipment and staging versus skin diving. He usually just floated along the surface and observed. He also found that he could cruise the eel grass beds, hovering just above their forest of plant matter and find four times as many crabs versus walking along the surface. He was below the polarizing mirror of the surface and could see them scurrying along in the eel grass.

The last time, he went crabbing floating through the eel grass, he discovered that not only could he panic, but that his body would take him a long way before his training would respond. He was swimming along in about two feet of water, peering through the eel grass, looking for the telltale reddish hues of crabs, when he came face to face with the ugliest fish he had ever seen. It had huge eyes and a mouth which was at least a half a foot wide. They looked at each other with what can only be interpreted as surprise and then the fish bolted for deep water and Ray found himself breathing hard and standing on the beach. He could hear Sophia laughing at his reaction. But he also knew that in any dangerous situation he knew that the beach would protect him, thank God.

Sophia has Competition

As Ray became a teenager, his thoughts turned to a more hormonal form of love. The area where Ray grew up was very rural, and a long way from any concentration of people. It took over two hours per day on a bus just to get to junior or senior high school. This was normally a very boring part of his day, and during the school year, took up almost all of the daylight hours. But he met a wonderful girl which had just moved into the general neighborhood (less than two miles away). When they learned that they shared an active dream life, where books, visions, and beliefs held sway versus who was going to be at the local dance, etc., they grew together in common feelings.

They would have long intimate discussions about life in general and their dreams for the future. Since everyone else their age was indifferent or did not understand these thoughts, they formed a tight friendship. As summer approached, they decided that they would do a project on the beach. They would build a raft out of the flotsam and jetsam which washed up on the beach. Ray began storing up large pieces of Styrofoam and planks to build the body of the raft. Ray was aware, that Sophia felt slighted by the attentions he was spending on this competitor for his time. Ray, full of raging hormones, dismissed her concerns and looked forward to a summer alone with the young lady.

Ray, as usual, did not comprehend the depths of Sophia's animosity and the friends which Sophia had at her disposal. Sophia, called upon the powers of the earth, and they had one of the first summers without a summer. For all of June and July, it rained every day. In August, the weather began to change to a warmer more normal pattern, but the young lady was required to spend three weeks in the San Juan Islands vacationing with her family and sailing through the islands. When she returned, the weather again turned nasty with almost continuous rain from late August throughout September. Thus, the entire summer was lost, and Ray and the girl remained friendly but drifted apart.

Ray agreed and went back to his daily conversations about life and his desires, with the only true friend he had ever known. Thus, Sophia and Ray continued with their relationship unfettered by any competition at all.

92

Ray's Boat, the Manatee
(Sea Cow)

In downtown Seattle, there was a world-famous sporting goods shop. If his family had time waiting for a ferry, they would sometimes stop there to browse. That's how they bought the telescope, while they were looking at decoys and other such stuff. The salesman sold his Dad on getting a telescope. It had five different lenses and was incredibly difficult to use, but they maintained a constant watch for ships, boaters and marine animals.

Several years later, they saw a dinghy at this store. Not only could it be rowed, but it had a small sail and outriggers to steady it in the stiff currents. The salesman once again saw an easy sale and convinced Ray's father that this was the boat to have.

One look at her underway in the Sound, and her name was born. Ray's parents thought that he would name it the Intrepid or Enterprise, but after one look at her under sail or oar power, brought Ray's mind to the ubiquitous sea cow, or Manatee. The manatee under sail garnered no speed records and in fact lived up to her name in both spirit and reality. The first time they attempted to sail her, his Dad was at the tiller and they sailed back and forth across the wind and despite their best efforts, were gradually swept backwards along the beach. The currents and the Manatee's flat bottom made for an impossible combination. They eventually had to beach her, take down the sail and row her back to where they stowed her on the logs. Ray's Dad was so disappointed; he never sailed again.

They eventually solicited the help of a superior sailor in our community. He helped them by pointing out that only one outrigger at a time should be in the water, since they increased drag. He taught them that the sail acted like an airplane wing and needed to be at a proper angle to pull them into the wind. The Manatee, would never be a world beater, but finally they could sail her upwind as long a strong current was not acting against her.

Setting up the sail, the tiller and the outriggers took about an hour, and so they rarely used it as a sailboat anyway and usually just rowed it around the beach. Ray thought one day about rowing across the Sound to the other side and set out in the Manatee to row on over. After an hour and a half, the other side looked just as distant as at the beginning but he was a long way out in the Sound and starting to get very tired. It was like walking in Las Vegas and seeing the next hotel and deciding that anyone could just walk on over there and then realizing that each hotel is one hell of a long way from their neighbors. Thank goodness, he turned around. By the time he got back into the beach, he climbed out of the boat and just lay in Sophia's arms for a half an hour to catch his breath.

Ray's Dad next saw a deal on an outboard motor and decided that they would buy it and use it to fish and put around the beach. It was only small outboard. To set it up, they had to lug the motor to the beach, along with the gas tank. This took about an hour to set up on the boat. Ray became very adept at setting up the boat on the logs where they kept it and then using all of his strength, shoving it over the logs and pushing it down the slope of the beach and into the water. He timed it so when the bow hit the water, he leaped inside and floated out into the bay. A quick couple of pulls on the rope and the engine would start. He had set up the engine to be straight along the line of the boat. Once inside the boat he climbed into the bow and with the engine gunning for all its worth, began steering the boat by just shifting his weight from one side to the other. Several years later, he worked in the marina in the nearby town, and he overheard a conversation between two boaters about this kid who used to live south of the marina. One of the boaters mentioned with considerable admiration that the boy would shove a boat from the logs directly into the water and roar off into the waves. Ray told them that it was he, and they spent an hour asking him about the reasons and how impressed they were when they had seen it so many times in the past.

Given his active dream life, when he was in the manatee, he envisioned that he was in a PT boat, with machine guns, mortars and torpedoes. His little boat was protecting the bases in the Sound from invasion and capture. Although standing in the bow of a ten-foot dinghy, moving at no more than 12-15 mph would seem ludicrous to any real Navy man; in his mind, it was a fast moving and dangerous defender of our society. From where he started, he could go the four miles along the shoreline into town or travel south and explore the northern reaches of other islands. Most of the time he would just go into town to bum around exploring his new found freedom.

One time he actually ventured into the ferry lanes and began circling back to the marina breakwater. He was still steering the boat by shifting his weight. To avoid crossing in front of the ferry, he decided to go through the dock support piling. Too late, he realized that he had seriously miscalculated both his rate of speed and the angle necessary to go through the support piling. He rammed the little boat into the piling going at full speed and almost tumbled out of the boat. He managed to grab hold of the gunwale at the last minute and just barely keep from going headfirst over the bow. The Manatee shivered to its core with the contact and Ray was sure that the impact had done serious damage to his little boat. Once docked in the marina, the boat checked out fine. The high-density plastic of the hull was not even bent by the impact. He was more shaken than his boat ever was. He walked around town for several hours before he returned to the boat for the trip home.

The Artist

Ray's mom never ceased in her efforts to bring culture and art into her family. Being an accomplished water color painter, she would work for days creating sketches or full paintings of the beach and dock. She was also searching for new ways to use what she and Ray found on the beach as art. They had collected quite a pile of driftwood with unusual shapes along with shells of unique clams and other animals.

One day after spotting an unusual color of glass shining in the beach rocks, she set upon a mission to collect multiple colors of glass and use them to make hurricane lanterns. The candles would shine through the sides of the lantern and the multiple shades and create a dazzling effect in a darkened room. Making these unique lanterns required them to constantly search for new glass fragments from the beach which could be used to make the colors burst forth. Although much of the glass was green or brown, weathering leached out some of the colors over time and created blues, subtle reds and finally the elusive purple glass.

When glass has spent years in saltwater and sun, it loses almost all of its color except for purple. Ray during his constant visits with Sophia, would always be on the lookout for glass, but especially the purples. Ray developed a permanent tendency to walk looking at the ground. For the rest of his life, he would always walk looking down at the ground, to find that elusive purple glass, even when he was in some strange city for a conference or travel, he would concentrate on what could be seen in a small area around his feet.

Also, since they were the most weathered, they allowed lighter to issue from the hurricane lanterns. While he searched for those elusive purple fragments, he discovered whole new areas to absorb his mind. He wondered what created the uniformity of the rocks in shape, which was flat and saucer shaped? Why did so many shells wash up on the shoreline? Could you make miniature liquor glasses by adding stems to cleaned and polished large barnacles? Why did so many logs wash up on the shore? And what marine animals existed below the rocks at every level of the beach?

Professor Durant had spent several weeks preparing his lecture and as he finished this section, he knew that the easy part was over. By opening up and discussing why he had learned as a child about oceanography, beach dynamics, and marine environments, he knew it would be controversial if not considered utterly insane. Now, he was contemplating confessing his own personal betrayal of Sophia and his failure to protect her. He had hidden it for years, and to now open up a wound which was over 50 years old, would be the most traumatic thing he had ever done.

He steeled himself to the effort and began to document the Mountain King's attack on Sophia and his efforts to save her. As Ray began to reflect on how this story would end, he tried to get a hold of Marcie. He desperately needed to get talk with her and have her help him overcome his fears of telling the world about this final chapter. After calling many times, without any response, he had his typist call from her cell phone. Marcie took that call out of curiosity. When she found out who it was from, she affirmed that she wanted nothing to do with him or the story. Afterward the secretary told him that she could hear the pain in her voice. He vowed to keep trying and had his secretary mail Marcie a special invitation to his lectures, hoping that she would forgive him when she listened to the whole story.

The Attack

The Bodyguards met periodically to monitor and discuss Ray's progress. They had watched as he went off to college, and they told Sophia, that in just a few more years, he would be the hero they needed to help defend them from humans and the Mountain King. He just needed his advanced degrees to be the expert they needed to discuss the importance of interrelationships and their impact on any environment.

The mountain king never forgot how he had been tricked by Sophia and her bodyguard. He knew that if he continued to wait, Ray would develop into the champion that Sophia would need to defend her from his vengeance. And he was jealous of her loving relationship with Ray. Finally, he could stand it no more and cried out loud, "Is there no one that can help me gain my vengeance upon this woman?" Within a day, a Rakon arrived and suggested that he had a plan to help the Mountain King. The King's jealousy blinded him to the ramifications involved and he decided that he had waited long enough for Sophia to come to her senses. Together, they developed a plan to attack Sophia, where she least expected it.

While the degaussing property was under federal control, it was off the tax rolls, and veiled from any other usage. After twelve years of caretaker status, the person in charge of maintaining the degaussing station was looking to retire. The residents along the beach began to solicit the Navy to turn the remaining structures into a park and let the County or State maintain the property for the good of everyone. But, in order to donate the property, it had to undergo a process of letting all of the other federal agencies decide if they wanted it, prior to moving the property out of federal control. Thus, the property was inherited by the GSA, which began to solicit ideas for its reuse. For some time, it was considered by a drug rehabilitation agency for use as a half-way house for recovering addicts. This got the whole community in an uproar, and was finally abandoned. Finally, the GSA determined that it could sell the property to the highest bidder and return it to normal usage. Ray's parents fought against this for almost five years, thinking that control of the property would devolve some prime real estate which had been used by everyone in some degree, to private property status.

Finally, they bowed to the inevitable. Ray had moved on to the University of Washington and was studying Oceanography, marine science, and chemistry. The GSA determined that in order to sell the property, the surface of the old dock must go. Typically, it is required to leave the support piling in place, to show that an existing structure had been demolished, and to keep the existing conditions on the beach relatively the same.

The community met to discuss what to do with the derelict dock and facility to make recommendations to the government concerning its ultimate disposal. Ray decided that he must attend to give a technical perspective of what should be done to protect the Sophia, which he was careful to say the "Beach environment". Over 90% of the people along the Beach attended, meeting in the old grange hall. The Government agents sat behind a series of tables on the old stage, while they listened wearily to each person as they stepped to the sole microphone at the head of the chairs in the hall.

One neighbor had taken the role as spokesperson for the property values along the beach. They wanted the old degaussing station returned as a park with road access to the beach for everyone. The government personnel stated unequivocally that this would not occur. If anything, the property would be sold at auction and returned to the State's tax rolls. Ray stood and talked to the issues of leaving as much of the areas as pristine as possible.

He convinced many in the audience, but the GSA asked one pertinent question; "Did he have any credentials to back up his claims to knowledge of how the environment would be impacted?"

When he announced, "I am only a student." The GSA ignored his pleas out of hand.

Within weeks, the GSA announced their decision. The property would be sold at auction. The dock would be torn down, but the piling would remain and no further discussions were anticipated.

Now the Mountain King's plan took final effect. As Ray returned to school, he had Rakon take on a reasonable human form. He assumed a human appearance and went down and talked to the contractor who was supposed to tear off the dock decking and remove it by barge. Sophia overheard one of his discussions with one of the people who lived along the cliffs.

Rakon started with the fact that no roads existed down to the shoreline. This meant a healthy slog down trails of stairs to the shore toting everything you might want on the beach, whether it was beer, marshmallows, or digging implements. He suggested how much better it would be to have a road right down to the beach, so you could pack everything up in a car and just drive down to a picnic area. He would even grant an easement to all the other owners to allow their use of the road. All he wanted was the piling from the dock piled up to cross the salt march and up the hillside to allow him to gravel a road into place. It all seemed so reasonable, but several facts were omitted. The piling had all been treated many years before with creosote, were actually hollow inside from the teredo worms, and the removal of the piling would change all of the environments which people so enjoyed. Sophia sought Ray, but he was away at college. She had no champion to dispute the demon's suggestions.

Speaking with such eloquence and reason, Rakon convinced many who heard him that he had everyone's best interest at heart. Knowing if she suspected his role with the Mountain King, Sophia would know how duplicitous his tongue was, he hid his aspect and spoke eloquently of the advantages of his ideas. That having a road to the beach would increase everyone's property values. As you can see, he worked on the avarice and self-interests of the other humans who lived along the beach. Rakon especially worked at convincing the demolition contractor that together they could work magic and reduce costs by following the King's plan.

Together, they decided it would be much easier to destroy all of the structure, and avoid the barging costs by building a road from the demon's property, across the salt march down to the beach. The demon even promised to make the road usable by anyone who lived along the shoreline. Everyone was happy that they would have immediate access to the beach by car, while the contractor was avoiding the costs of barging the materials away.

Sophia had some trepidation about this solution, and Ray had just taken several courses that illustrated the dangers of this approach. By taking rotting timbers, coated with creosote, and dumping them into the salt march, they essentially killed the salt marsh, removing and entire eco system from the beach. No more frogs, pollywogs or ducks stayed in the area. The piling left all rolled up into a long road-like structure, quickly rotted and within a year, the road was gone. The removal of the piling, completely removed the fish habitats, and affected the long-shore currents which had produced the sand bars and tidal pools. The seagulls lost their nesting sites and moved away, to be replaced by hundreds of Ravens, and their raucous calls.

Ray knew esoterically about the damage this solution would cause, but he could never get anyone to listen to what the long-term effects would be. He was away at the University of Washington, and he rarely had time to come back to see his love. But one summer he went back to the beach where he learned so much about life and love. He saw now the immensity of the destruction of the old dock and what the greed of a single human had done with the decking and the piling. By removing not just the decking, but also the piling, the fish environment had disappeared totally, taking the perch, rock cod, and flounder with it. The sand bar and tidal pool quickly disappeared taking the sea-pens and geoducks. By piling the decaying logs in the salt marsh to build a road from the bluff to the beach, the salt marsh was destroyed. With the fish, the seagulls, the frogs and the sandbar gone, much of Sophia's power went with them.

She felt the loss of so many of her beloved friends. Eagle left first, because the fish stocks had diminished drastically, Crab went next, claiming that without the sandbars and eel grass environment his homes were destroyed. Octopus retreated to the depths. The only one remaining was Raven, who had managed to find a way to survive in any human environment. Raven met with Sophia, who was gradually losing all vitality.

Raven admired her for the last time, and then said "I had no idea how cunning the Mountain King was, I failed you by not anticipating how he would use humans to destroy so much life so quickly.

Sophia smiled wanly, and said, "You have never failed me. No one could have known how devious and destructive the Mountain King would be. Please do one last favor for me and seek out Ray and tell him to see me soon, before I completely fade away."

Raven flew off that minute and arrived at Ray's bedroom window and spoke to him with urgency in his voice. He tried hard to avoid placing blame on Ray, but his sarcasm about Ray's priorities and how he had abandoned his lifelong friend came shining through. Ray was ashamed of having left her alone for so long, and went home the next day to see her.

Ray returned home from school and immediately went down to see her. She usually had been right there when he arrived, but now he couldn't find her at all. He walked the logs of the beach and finally found here curled up between two of the favorite logs. She looked sad and weak, with a corona which ebbed and flowed with the waves, was all that could be seen. At first, he thought he had changed and was no longer attuned to her soul. He sat down on the logs and pondered his lack of effort to maintain their relationship. As he meditated, he began to barely hear her voice again.

*She said, "I feel tired and lonely and I am sorry that
I cannot speak as I once was. My friends have left me,
all except for you."*

Quickly he responded with his love for her and was their anything he could do to help. Even though he knew in his heart that the removal of the dock had doomed her and he had done nothing to prevent it.

*Her only response was, "I don't know why I feel
diminished and small, but I still love you with all my
heart. Why have you been gone for so long?"*

Feeling a pit of guilt grow in his stomach, he turned to anger to avoid his responsibility.

*He practically screamed back at her, "You never
understood about all of my needs! I never learned
how to interact with other girls, now I have found
many relationships that are much more physically
satisfying. I was making up for all my lost time."*

Now she felt the pangs of guilt, realizing that she should have offered him a more complete relationship, instead of using him for her own purposes. Rather than respond she accepted his tirade, but her pride made her turn away.

Ray left vowing to find out what he could do to save her.

Even after his promise to help Sophia, he had to spend several years away at graduate school. He was required to spend an inordinate amount of time at sea. The school's area of concentration was the Bering Sea, which had both similarities and major differences from his beach. He began to concentrate on the interactions between marine organisms and how those relationships grew with the environment. As the niches increased for the marine organisms, the newer species joined the area. When he returned to as a lecturer, he prepared his observations for a series of lectures for marine biology and oceanography students. Finally, he returned to tell her of the success of his lectures.

This time could not raise her spirit to communicate. It was if her voice was stilled. He forced himself to meditate on his errors and sat on the logs for several hours. He finally heard her voice weakly as if from far away.

*"As the Mountain King foretold, I am dying", was
all she said.*

*He cried, "Please don't go. All my other relationships
never last more than a few weeks or months, I need
you.'*

*Her response, "Where were you when I needed
you?"*

*He responded, "I was a young upstart, no one
would have listened to me anyway."*

Her tone was filled with remorse, "But did you try?"

His understanding was surpassed only by the guilt he felt by concentrating on his own life and leaving her to struggle alone with the devastation.

He realized that she was right, that even though he was personally very successful he had failed her when she needed him most, and the knowledge tore at his soul. He decided at that time, to do whatever was necessary to make her memory live on and that the rewards she deserved would finally come to her.

*Her final reflection to Ray was, "I loved you and love
you still. Remember me when I was strong and*

*vibrant and teach others what you know now. That
will be enough, do not blame yourself for my death,
it would have come anyway. I need you to wreak my
final vengeance upon the Mountain King. Knowing I
am weakened, he will arrive and try to possess me as
his personal slave and concubine. He will threaten
you, bluster at you, and finally offer you a worldly
fortune. You must hold out but finally acquiesce and
tell him this certain date, that I trust only to you. You
will tell him then, that I have gone into hiding where
he least expects it. Tell him I am hiding in the
dungeons of his old palace on Mount Saint Helens.
Good Bye and I love you."*

He whispered, "And I love you".

He asked her why that particular date was so important, but
her voice was stilled. He vowed that her memory would live in every
lecture he ever gave and he would show her passion for life.

As Ray walked along the beach where he had shared so much life
and learning with her, he caught himself staring at his feet as he walked.
The tears which coursed down his cheeks, were hot and salty. Just then
he looked up, and could see a man walking towards him, wearing a
white suit. As he looked closer, he noticed the back van dyke beard and
the hard cold eyes staring back at him.

As they met, the Mountain King grabbed him by the upper
arms and held him in his vise like grip. Ray wanted to call out to the
bodyguards, but realized that they had all gone, with the death of
Sophia.

*The Mountain king looked intently into his eyes and said,
"You were nothing to fear, even when she and her friends
were around. Now you are just a pitiful weak human. I
could tear you in half easily."*

*Ray responded by staring into those hard eyes and said, "Go
ahead, do what you want!"*

*He knew he must use all his wiles to capture the Mountain
King's interest. your worst.'*

"If I do, I will never find her. You know where she is? Don't you." said the Mountain King.

"Yes, but you will never find her!" Ray challenged.

The Mountain King's response was quick, "Tell me where she is and I will let you live."

"Never!" was his only response.

The Mountain King saw his resolve and decided to use his wiles to make him an offer, "No, that would be too easy. Right now, you want to die, rather than live with your betrayal. Instead, I will offer all my resources to make you the leading expert in the land. All people will defer to you in the future and you will be able to protect her realm as well as she ever did."

The Mountain King, thought he understood all humans, and that this offer would buy him Sophia and allow him to turn her into his personal slave and concubine. Later he would break this upstart human just as he had Sophia.

Ray looked pensive and finally disingenuously agreed to tell him her hiding place. He told him that she had gone to hide in his old palace.

The Mountain King let out a shout of joy, grabbed Rakon and shot into the air and flew back to the mountain. He had blocked all of the entrances except two years ago.

He stationed Rakon at one end and began to search the castle. As he descended into the depths, he began to sense more and more shaking as a series of minor earthquakes shook the castle. But he forged ahead rejoicing that he at last would have his vengeance upon the woman who had rejected him. At that point, the very Mountain beneath the feet began to shift and then explode. As he descended into the pit created, the Mountain King realized that immortality in the fiery depths, he saw fast approaching, was a hefty payment indeed for his vengeance.

As he put the finishing touches on his lecture series, he knew that the Dean would never let him give it as he planned. The Dean was both crafty and cunning and would find some way to get his lectures ahead of time and find a way to stop their presentation. Professor

Durant thought about how to cope with this issue. He decided to call in a few markers. He had met and shared a few beers at conferences with both Dr. Ballard and the son of Jacque Cousteau. He had their cell phones tucked away on his contact list. He called them up and asked them to read at least the first few pages of his planned lecture. When he sent it off to them, he did not tell his secretary or anyone else of these contacts. He hoped that they would read the initial couple of lectures and become intrigued with his story. He got more than that, both called back and wanted to meet with him and come to the first lecture series. They also suggested that as a group the approach the Discovery and Science Channels to see if they were interested in a story about the inspiration of many scientists.

He agreed to meet with them, but not on his campus. They met in New York and the Discovery Channel not only showed some interest, they were willing to film the lecture series and use portions of it in a special. Michael Cousteau even mentioned that his father had told a very similar story to him as a fairy tale when he was young. At least he thought it was a fairy tale until now.

The Discovery Channel had not only contacted Dr. Ballard and Mr. Cousteau, but many other scientists and found that most of them had similar stories to relate how a muse came to set them on their path to field of expertise.

Now that he had an insurance plan set up, Professor Durant proceeded to give the last pieces of the story to the secretary. When he delivered the last pages, he stood up. When he heard her gently weeping in the other room, he went to the doorway, and she looked up from the last pages, with tears streaming down her cheeks.

He asked, "What's wrong?"

She sobbed, "I never knew, no one did...and I may have made a serious mistake."

Before he could respond, she looked at him for a long time, and finally said, "If you change even one word of this lecture, I will never forgive you. I don't care what the Dean thinks; it is marvelous just as you have told it."

The very next day, he walked into his office and the secretary was staring at the surface of the desk. The only thing she said was, "The Dean is waiting for you inside."

As Professor Durant stepped over the threshold, the dean's fearsome and sharp featured face grinned at him as he barely looked up from the papers he was holding.

He said, "A very interesting story, but I can't let you tell it."

"Oh, and why not" was the professor's response. "I recall that you told me you would not censor my lectures at all!"

The Dean looked up from the chair, and leaned back to say –

"I can't have you embarrass me, yourself or this University by publicly exposing a serious mental defect with this fantastical story of yours. I have worked too long to build up the credentials of this department and get Government funding to have it all undone by a crazy story such as this."

The Professor looked back and rebutted –

"You never did understand the importance of a calling, did you? How did you get the secretary to give you my complete lecture?"

"She found it relatively easy to betray you once I offered a full graduate school scholarship." was his response.

"I knew that she was weak, but I never thought she would betray me so cheaply." he countered. "It is a good thing I had a back-up plan for just this contingency."

"What do you mean?" the Dean returned.

The professor held up a series of letters. "I just

received the final response from several dignitaries who plan on attending. I even shared some of the gist of my lectures. Surprisingly enough almost all said they had a life changing event which had also led them to pursue their careers. None, mention Sophia, but they loved the story and are planning on attending. Professor Ballard, Michael Cousteau and the Discovery channel even plan to do a feature documentary and use me as the technical advisor and contributor. The current working title is "Muses of Science". They think it will help the general public to understand more of the creative and scientific methods. I think they would react poorly to a cancellation of my lectures series."

The Dean visibly paled and he stammered out one last shot –

"Let's not be too hasty, no one is talking about cancelling the series, just a softening of some of the more mystical elements."

The professor responded, "I plan to give the lecture just as it is written and to hell with your issues."

The Dean bowed his head, and stumbled from the office, knowing that he was beaten.

The very next week, he began the lectures series. It was a hit with invitees, students and faculty. The Dean was visibly absent, which did not hurt his feelings at all. At the end of the lecture series, he talked about his great love and how he had failed to protect her. These lectures were his personal penance for his neglect at a critical time. He found that people responded to this passion for her in many ways. It was rare that the tears that welled up his eyes were not mirrored throughout the audience.

Marcie had not planned on attending his lectures, but then she had received a hand written invitation asking her to please come. She had thought about it for several weeks, not sure if she wanted to open old wounds, but she finally decided to come and hear him speak.

On the final day of the lecture series, he received a standing ovation as he related the final days of Sophia. Marcie, in particular was affected by his story of Sophia's death. She could see the catharsis in his soul and realized that it had changed him, when he related the story. As tears started down her cheeks, she began to get up to leave the hall. At that precise moment, he looked up in the back of the hall, and could see her standing alone. He motioned for her to join him. When she arrived, he grabbed her about the waist and twirled her around, expressing his joy at seeing her again.

She said, "I knew you were a spellbinder, but what a story."

He looked into her eyes for a long moment and said –

"I have finally made amends for the sins of my youth. My nightmares ended last week. Would you consider taking me on as your worshiper?"

She looked just as deeply into his eyes and said –

"I don't need a worshipper. I need a flesh and blood man with passion, experience and integrity. I finally found him under my very nose. Maybe it's time for us both to really visit the Dalmation Coast on cruise."

He nodded and his smile was genuine. He was truly happy for the first time in many years. They walked off the stage together arm in arm.

Epilogue

As with anyone who has ever failed and was then offered a chance at redemption, Ray Durant became a champion for keeping some environments unsullied, pristine and life fulfilling. He testified before congress concerning the reasons and the need for Environmental Impact Statements (EIS) After many years of striving for the seemingly impossible, EIS are now required before any construction or demolition. With those laws in place, you can now find so many areas, surrounding a major metropolitan area such as Seattle, with pristine and growing life environments which are not sculptured and maintained as parks to some dream of perfection. From the old growth forest of the Grove of the Patriarchs to isolated beaches in the Sound, life goes on growing and creating without man's help, beyond any conviction to not meddle.

He became even more famous as a lecturer at the University and throughout the remainder of his life; he taught not only facts and knowledge, but the need to fully understand the impacts of change. He found that these lectures began to grow beyond the immediate attendance to include people who wanted to hear his stories and recognized his passion for the soul mate he had lost and the life of every constituent on earth. He began each lecture series with a version of the Louis Armstrong song.

"It's a Wonderful World"

The seaweeds of green, red tides too,
I see them grow, for me and for you.
And I think to myself, What a wonderful world I see
seas of blue, Beaches of white.
The bright blessed day
And the pale, moonlit night. And I think to myself,
What a wonderful world

He brought the passion of Sophia to the forefront in every discussion and was always a staunch defender of knowing all of the impacts prior to decisions being made. He required his students concentrate on the interrelationships being the key to a healthy environment. The main feature was that humans could no longer consider themselves as somehow separate from the world. So that Sophia's legacy will always be intact, that we are caretakers and not just residents of the only home we will ever know. Thus, the loss of even a single species places us that much closer to the end of our home and of us.

duct-compliance